Strategies for the Tech-Savvy Classroom

Strategies for the
Tech-Savvy
Classroom

Diane Witt

Routledge
Taylor & Francis Group

NEW YORK AND LONDON

First published 2009 by Prufrock Press Inc.

Published 2021 by Routledge
605 Third Avenue, New York, NY 10017
2 Park Square, Milton Park, Abingdon, Oxon OX14 4RN

Routledge is an imprint of the Taylor & Francis Group, an informa business

Cover and Layout Design by Marjorie Parker

ISBN 13: 978-1-59363-356-1 (pbk)

Dedication

This book is dedicated to my parents, who taught me never to give up; my husband, for his love, encouragement, and sense of humor throughout this project; Meredith, who taught me about technology; and Erin, who has always been my inspiration!

Contents

Acknowledgements ix

Introduction xi

Part I: Becoming a Tech-Savvy Classroom 1

    Chapter 1: Net Smart and Safe: Number One Priority Online 3

    Chapter 2: Ethics and Cyberethics. 15

    Chapter 3: Online Technologies: Playgrounds for Tech-Savvy Kids . . 25

    Chapter 4: Combining Technology and Simulations 61

    Chapter 5: Telementoring, Virtual Teams, and Distance Learning. . . .67

    Chapter 6: Advocating for the Tech-Savvy Student 87

Part II: Facilitating High-Interest Learning 91

    Animal Writings. 96

    Endangered Species 102

    Jamestown: An Historical Role Play. 116

    False Faces 123

    States Within the U.S.: Making Connections:. 130

    Shapes Are All Around Us. 135

    Digital Vocabulary. 140

    Making History 145

    Stop Motion Pro 151

    Images of Deceit. 158

    Creating a Utopian Society. 166

    References 175

    About the Author 181

    About the Contributors. 183

Acknowledgements

This project has been about making connections. It has been about the teachers, the parents, and—most of all—the kids and their passion for technology.

The lessons were contributed by Angela Ardoin, Sandra Cookson, Jeri-Lyn Flowers, Sharon Leamy, David W. McDivitt, Debra Parkes, Kim Poe, Cindy Sheets, Kenneth J. Smith, Ph.D., Eppie Snider, Rob Stetson, and Craig Wargowsky. Their lessons are a snapshot of the some of the creative ways technology is being used in our schools. These teachers have shared their stories and their insights. Most of all, their lessons reflect the energy and devotion they have for the students they serve and the field in which they teach. Their efforts are greatly appreciated.

I also want to thank the following people for their valuable information and advice:
- Mary Ellen Amaral Carras (Town Hall Lecture Series),
- Dr. Mary Christopher (online discussion forums),
- Zac Burson (telementoring),
- Liz Pape (Virtual High School),
- Dr. Parry Aftab (Internet safety),
- Jason Hubbard (educaching),
- Sue Heckler and Nicole Williams (e-portfolios),
- Dr. Steve Rapp (Lin Holton Governor's School),
- Dr. Del Siegle (telementoring),
- Kelly Szarneki (Teen Second Life),
- Eric Calvert,

- Sister Rosemary Hug,
- Muriel Summers,
- Dr. Thomas Southern, and
- Craig Wargowsky and his talented art students.

They have taught me a lot, and you can hear echoes of their work throughout out this book.

Numerous people shared their guidance and provided support along the way. They provided the motivation to follow through with this endeavor. Heartfelt gratitude goes to Rondell Belt, Nancy Bosch, Liz and Liv Campochiaro, Nanci Christie, Lisa and Daisy Dias, Janie Hobson-Dupont, Jackie Jettie, Sandy Oliver, Linda Somers, Carolyn Thayer, Sandra Warren, Jean Watts, and Brian Whitener. A special thanks also goes to Steve Simons for his technical assistance.

A number of teachers and administrators took the time to fill out questionnaires about technology. A special thanks goes to Janet Kirchoff and the Houston County gifted program teachers in the elementary, middle school, and high school honors and AP classes and the enrichment pull-out class from Warner Robins, GA. I'd also like to thank the teachers from Glenburn Elementary School in Glenburn, ME, and the Massachusetts Association for Gifted Education for their help. In addition, teachers from Florida and Ohio answered the questionnaires as well, and I'd like to thank them for their contribution.

I also want to mention my editor, Jennifer Robins, for her support throughout this project, and Prufrock Press for giving me a chance to put my thoughts on paper.

Most of all, I want to thank my daughter, Erin. I couldn't have done this without you!

Introduction

"It is not our abilities that show what we truly are. It is our choices."
—Professor Dumbledore to Harry Potter in *Harry Potter and the Chamber of Secrets* (Rowling, 1999)

You were probably interested in this book because you, like the students you teach, are fascinated, immersed, and hooked on technology. Quite often, our students may know more about technology than we do, and we find ourselves wondering what we can do to keep their attention and stay ahead of their rapidly expanding knowledge.

This generation of students is connected by cell phones, iPods, text messaging, and social networks. They are bloggers and content creators. They share photos and videos, plan parties, and manipulate information—all electronically! Finding a way to nurture that passion and embrace these young digital citizens is no small task. These students learn differently and see things in ways we never will.

Watching children succeed and develop a passion for a subject has always been an integral part of my life. As a parent and an educator, I realized that the moment a child achieved an "a-ha!" moment on any topic, from sports to music to technology, the success empowered him or her to continue.

This book had its beginnings on the small island of Nantucket. I never realized the importance of technology until I met a young woman who was fascinated with the topic. She loved everything about the Internet, C++ programming, and JavaScript. She talked about them constantly and was always checking out ways that she could conquer the newest technologies. She was an avid reader, and was well aware when new technology products were coming on the market.

None of these things really meant too much to me at the time, but for her, technology was a lifeline that reflected the way she learned. It bridged the gap between traditional forms of learning and what she understood. Until we (meaning educators) allowed her to lead the way, she failed miserably. Once we began viewing her technological skill as a strength, technology was integrated into her regular classroom assignments, and her achievement started on an upward swing. Her schooling experience went from failing to thriving.

Strategies for the Tech-Savvy Classroom is an effort to inspire teachers who can take these students to levels only they can understand. It is about allowing alternatives for gifted and advanced students with technology talent who need a teacher who can provide a technology-rich environment to enhance those skills.

The book is divided into two sections. The first section offers information on safety and ethics, in addition to providing a growing list of emerging technologies and how they can be applied to the classroom. The first section also includes information on advocating for these tech-savvy students. One of the reasons I wrote *Strategies for the Tech-Savvy Classroom* was because more and more students are entering our schools tech-ready with new understandings and ways to communicate their knowledge.

The second section contains a collection of lessons from teachers highlighting the ways they use technology to promote higher level thinking skills, independent thinking, and creativity. These lessons, which are aligned with national standards, are a snapshot of what teachers are doing across the country to incorporate technology into the curriculum and promote this kind of rich learning environment.

I want to invite you to a classroom where kids come to school dreaming of taking part in "code jams" or creating the next World of Warcraft. These participatory learners are pioneering ways of learning that require new strategies for the classroom.

The challenge is ours. Won't you please help us reach it?

—Diane Witt

PART I

Becoming a
Tech-Savvy Classroom

Net Smart and Safe: Number One Priority Online

"Exploration, knowledge, and achievement are only as good as we determine how to use them."

—John Glenn

STUDENTS in language arts class were just completing *Ender's Game* (Card, 2002), a science-fiction novel that had become popular and was soon to become a movie. Set in the future, Andrew "Ender" Wiggin was "selected" to become a future military commander because of his intellectual genius. Children were identified at a young age, and by 6, Ender was on his way to Battle School, where only the smartest were groomed and chosen to protect the future.

More than a study in literature, the book also offers the writer's perceptions of giftedness in a future world and confronts some challenges already being faced in our technologically driven society. One of these hurdles is the cyberbully. In the novel, a cyberbully harassed Ender until he manipulated the school's security system to create a student who did not exist. When he did, he outwitted his adversary and stopped the bullying.

This book opened a dialogue for teachers in a local community that had experienced its share of pranks and threats to students using the Internet, despite its attempts to monitor student use. Because the school was protected with filtering software that blocked access to certain sites, students' activity could be monitored. The school also implemented an acceptable use policy that explained what was considered appropriate and inappropriate online activity. Parents and students were required to sign the agreement, and teachers were allowed and urged to check students' personal CD-ROMs for inappropriate content.

The Internet is the largest library of information available. Billions of pages exist and have expanded the opportunities for the way children learn. Therefore, Internet literacy is necessary to succeed in school and the workplace. Unfortunately, there will always be those who will abuse the technology. Making students more aware of the risks is part of the solution.

Children and the Internet

Younger and younger children are being introduced to the computer and the Internet. For example, Knowledge Adventure software promotes computer games to play with babies who are sitting on a parent's lap, just one of many types of "lapware" available. Early exposure to computer use also should reinforce safety issues when they are easiest to learn.

By the time children are between the ages of 4 and 7, watching mom and dad click from one site to another has become commonplace. At this age, many children are already using the computer, usually under the watchful eye of their parents. Although the majority of them are not avid readers yet, most young children have watched their parents navigate the Web, and eagerly try to imitate what they have watched. Four- and 5-year-olds are even able to play basic computer games just by following a simple icon.

During the "tween years" (ages 8–12), a child's perceptions of his or her world begins to change. Peer acceptance takes priority and tweens acquire a sense of independence about computer usage. At both school and home, a student with navigational skills and a sense of adventure may need closer monitoring of his or her activities.

Preteens (ages 12–14) often are busy online connecting with others. Most of them have been using the Internet for years, and are at ease with the technology and its advantages. Many have their own cell phones and are avid text messagers. Their familiarity with technology, however, also can lead to poor judgment issues at home and school, such as chatting with someone they don't know, planning meetings with strangers, and sharing personal information, such as their name, address, and phone number. Sometimes these students are quiet regarding their activity, which makes knowledge of Internet safety even more important.

During this time, sexual development also may trigger fantasy and interest. Because some sites can be extremely explicit, creating an open dialogue that recognizes a preteens' interests may make monitoring at this age easier—but not always. Monitoring software can be installed at home and school, but encouraging children to make safe choices about the sites they visit is still preferred. Although awareness forces them to think about the sites they've discovered, many students still have difficulty determining whether a Web site is valid or not.

School Concerns

Schools face a number of technological issues. The Children's Internet Protection Act of 2001 (PL 106-554) required schools to certify they have a safety policy. Filtering programs are used by schools to protect students from pornographic and unauthorized sites. These software products have become increasingly sophisticated and are able to detect if someone is trying to disable it or uninstall it. Even students with advanced technological abilities will have difficulty trying to circumvent these filters. Many have a "tamper detection" feature that has the ability to cut off Internet usage if a "breach" occurs (Willard, n.d.). Blocking technology denies access to sites that are harmful to children and monitors their activity. Although these safeguards have created more secure systems, schools continue to face ongoing concerns, including some of the ones listed below.

- *Inappropriate Language*—Teaching students to be responsible for their actions is not an easy thing—especially when what they do is protected by anonymity. Schools expect a standard of behavior from their students, online and off. Attacking another's character should not be allowed. Obscenity and prejudicial remarks toward others should not be tolerated. Language that causes anxiety in others or causes them to feel threatened in any way also is unacceptable. These policies urge students to think twice about what and how they communicate with others online.
- *Plagiarism and Copy Infringement*—Access to the Internet has made it easy for students to take another author's idea and use it as their own. Reproducing someone else's work without permission can result in copyright infringement for works protected by copyright, and this should be thoroughly discussed with students before they are given online access.
- *Pen Pal Programs*—Although pen pal programs are a great opportunity to connect with other children from different parts of the world, safeguards should be taken. Children should never share their full name or give out personal infor-

mation about their family. Passwords that allow students to play Internet games or take part in chat rooms should be kept private. In addition, children should never exchange photos or share any information that links them to their true identity, including the name of their school or hometown.

- *Privacy Issues*—Students have become very creative in their use of technology and have learned ways of getting around the system to pull pranks on some of their peers. Posting false information about someone is viewed as a great way to get back, and if it is done anonymously, it can be a lot of fun to kids. One tactic is to attach a picture of someone's face on another body. Another tactic is to send an e-mail over and over again to the same person. These behaviors are unacceptable and do not have a place in the classroom. Such behavior should be handled at the same level as non-Internet bullying or invasions of privacy.

It is not surprising that teens take the Internet seriously. According to a Pew Internet and American Life Study (Rainie, 2008), approximately 94% of teens in the 12–17 age group are online. Of these, 73% have broadband connection at home, 71% have their own cell phone, and 71% have a wireless connection (Rainie, 2008). In a recent study, OTX (2008), a global consumer research and consulting firm, did research into the lives teens lead online. They found that teens spend an average of 11.5 hours online a week, and this number increases if their computer is located in their bedroom.

Teens are using other types of technology as well. Cell phone usage has increased. Disney Mobile and Harris Interactive released a survey noting that teens are spending around 3 hours and 45 minutes a day on their cell phones, and according to Jupiter Research, around 24 % of kids between the ages of

10 and 11 have their own cell phones, and 38% of teens 12 and older have one (Olsen, 2006).

High-tech socializing has taken teens out of the mall and to fewer dances, but friends are never far away as a result of instant messaging, text messaging, cell phones, and PDAs. They are doing the things teens have always done, but in a slightly different format—one that utilizes technology.

However, the Internet also has a darker side. People from all walks of life contribute to and lurk on the Internet, and unfortunately some have agendas that are designed to victimize children. Educators need to be aware of the safety issues that may arise for students while using the Internet and should take steps to help prevent any breach of possible safety in their classrooms and schools.

Teaching in today's tech-savvy classroom is no easy task. Students know their way around the computer, are curious as to what is out there, and many want to test their own capabilities. As an educator, you must be proactive by partnering with parents and making students understand that there are safety rules in place to help keep them protected. The Internet is there for everyone and the risks should not overshadow its advantages.

Teachers need to stress the importance on being safe online on a regular basis. When a student is having fun and realizing the possibilities the computer can offer, it is hard to think of any consequences associated with it. To many, it's a game, but they need to understand the gravity of the situation if they break the rules.

High school students can be technologically sophisticated beyond their teachers and parents. Because cell phones, text messaging, the Internet, and PDAs are commonplace, adolescents who consider themselves to be proficient users find it difficult to understand that the online world can pose any danger to them.

Educator Concerns

No doubt about it—children and adults have never been freer to express their opinions, good or bad, through the Internet. With the advent of cyberbullying, online gaming, and social networking sites, students are more at risk than ever online. Teachers should be aware of potential safety issues, and be prepared to help students as needed.

Cyberbullying

> Cyber bullying involves the use of information and communication technologies such as e-mail, cellular phone and text messaging, defamatory personal websites and defamatory online personal polling websites to support deliberate repeated and hostile behavior to an individual or group that is intended to harm others. (Belsey, n.d., para. 1)

Most cyberbullying occurs between the ages of 9 and 14 and takes place after school. It's the most effective way to create nasty rumors about or send embarrassing pictures of other students. It creates the element of surprise that children can use anywhere, anytime. In most cases, bullies send their messages without fear of being caught, and also feel they are not responsible for any consequences of their actions (Belsey, n.d.). A lot of children who are being bullied choose not to inform their parents for fear they will take away their computer. The Mind Oh Foundation (http://www.mindohfoundation.org), an e-learning company that promotes character development, found that boys and girls could be both victims and bullies, and because 50% of kids are online without adult supervision, victims are easy to reach.

High-tech bullying has taken on a face of its own, and seems to be growing as children find more creative ways to get back at one another. Cyberbullying can take place without a parent's or teacher's knowledge. Unfortunately, many adults aren't aware that children are being bullied by cell phone texts, instant messaging, personal Web sites, and e-mail.

Online Gaming

As an integral part of the growing culture of people who frequent hot spots and Internet Cafes to connect with others, online gaming is on the rise. Although they spend much of their time interacting online, these gamers also meet IRL (in real life) to exchange tactics, watch others play, and compare strategies.

Online games are available for children as young as 3, and can be played as soon as a child can handle a mouse. The gaming world is more than a one-on-one experience. It has grown to global games, such as EverQuest II, which has more than 300,000 players worldwide, or World of Warcraft, which has more than 8 million players.

New technologies have made online gaming an exciting experience. They are more interactive and players become immersed in the games. These "live chat games" go on for all hours of the night and day.

As young children become better at gaming, predators keep their watch. They remain in the background and start to track certain children, waiting to obtain their trust. Even with precautions, interactive gaming allows children to speak online using their own voice. Within no time, the conversation can lead to an innocent exchange of a telephone number and address. A quick search on MapQuest can lead a stranger to a home (P. Aftab, personal communication, September, 2005).

That sharing of information also can extend to the classroom and provides concern for children's safety. Any child who will provide their home address also is likely to include information about his or her school, teacher, and location. What kids do online at home can affect what takes place at school. Safety is ongoing and parent–teacher partnerships can keep dialogues open. Wired Safety (http://www.WiredSafety.org) is a worldwide organization run by volunteers to help keep kids safe online and is a good resource for parents and educators alike.

Social Networking Sites

Social networking sites such as MySpace and Facebook are common arenas for today's teens to meet and interact with one another. Growing in popularity, they provide an ideal way for teens and young adults to share personal information. These sites also are being used to do homework, collaborate on projects, and share content with friends, making these sites popular to meet a student's educational and personal needs.

Although these sites are part of a teenager's daily life, there are still some risks. Membership is growing faster than the ability to screen members. MySpace is taking steps to protect its members. They are deleting inappropriate images and working with law enforcement agencies to remove sex offenders from the site. They also have started working with http://www. WiredSafety.org to provide online safety to their members and removing anyone that does not meet the 14 years of age minimum. However, it is very important for both educators and parents to teach students to be safe while on these, and all, Web sites.

Potential Classroom Issues and Suggestions

Although many schools have Internet filters and other measures to help restrict the content students access while on the Internet, "other strategies include educating children as early as possible about the benefits and dangers of using the Internet" (Australian Government NetAlert, 2007, p. 3). Teachers should be aware of the potential dangers the Internet can pose and be prepared to offer strategies to help students stay as safe as possible while on the computer.

Potential Internet safety issues for students include:
- exposure to inappropriate material,
- physical danger,
- financial risk,
- harassment and bullying,
- privacy,
- unreliable information,
- spam, and
- viruses (Australian Government NetAlert, 2007).

It is important to discuss safety rules prior to allowing students online access in the classroom. Most schools have acceptable use policies in place regarding technology, and teachers should ensure that every student understands the rules. In addition to reviewing the school's online policy, teachers should help students learn to distinguish between appropriate and inappropriate sites. This is especially important for younger students, as they may not be aware of how to discern whether a Web site is "good" or "bad." One way to control which sites children view is to identify a specific set of sites they can visit and then allow them to explore those and look at each site's characteristics.

Another way to improve children's online safety is to teach children how to search using search engines and keywords (Australian Government NetAlert, 2007). For elementary students, a few alternative "kid safe" search engines are recommended (Schneider, 2008), including:

- Yahoo! Kids (http://kids.yahoo.com),
- Ask Kids (http://www.askkids.com),
- KidsClick! (http://www.kidsclick.org),
- Google's SafeSearch for Kids (http://www.squirrelnet.com/search/Google_SafeSearch.asp), and
- Awesome Library (http://www.awesomelibrary.org).

Schneider (2008) also offers tips to help kids develop more efficient and safer searches. When entering keywords, students should:

- use correct spelling,
- use root words to retrieve multiple word endings (e.g., *teen* retrieves teens, teenagers, etc.),
- place quotation marks around a phrase, and
- use Boolean logic. (p. 30)

No matter how much time is spent discussing cybersafety in the classroom, there are times when students will come across content that is inappropriate. They should be equipped with effective procedures for removing themselves from the situation as soon as possible. These include:

- using the "back" button to exit the site,

- exiting the browser,
- clicking home, or
- turning off the monitor (Australian Government NetAlert, 2007, p. 10).

The following Web sites contain additional information about online safety for students, teachers, and parents.

- Center for Safe and Responsible Internet Use (http://www.csriu.org)
- Connect Safely! (http://www.connectsafely.org)
- Cybercitizen Awareness Program (http://www.cybercitizenship.org)
- CyberSmart! Student Curriculum (http://www.cybersmartcurriculum.org)
- GetNetWise (http://www.getnetwise.org)
- i-SAFE Inc. (http://www.isafe.org)
- NetSmartz (http://www.netsmartz.org)
- SafeKids.com (http://www.safekids.com)
- SafeTeens.com (http://www.safeteens.com)

Keeping ahead of a child who acts as the technician in the family isn't easy. For gifted students—and all students in the classroom—the emphasis is not on their ability to use the technology, but on ensuring their safety. Parents and educators must work together to help them channel their energies in the right direction and encourage safety at the same time.

Ethics and Cyberethics

"The significant problems we face cannot be solved at the same level of thinking we were at when we created them."

—Albert Einstein

THE teacher of the second-grade gifted program had spent some time introducing her students to the computer. For Chris, it equaled hours of entertainment and excitement. Even at the young age of 7, he was fascinated with the things it could do. He was an avid reader and devoured everything he could to increase his understanding. That ability allowed him to write his first computer program—in the second grade.

By the time he was 12, he knew his way around the computer and had become proficient at using the Internet. Therefore, it really was not surprising when he and his friend were able to break into the Web site of a major corporation. Chris had become a hacker (Schwartau, 2001). By age 15, Chris knew he wanted to work in computer security, and by age 18, he had formed his own security company. Today, Chris is a recognized expert on issues that pertain to information security.

Cyberethics and the Classroom

Simply defined, ethics boil down to choices, and making the right decision. Those using the Internet also are held to an ethical standard. Cyberethics concern responsible and ethical behavior while online (Cybercitizenship.org, n.d.). Because so many people are online, cyberethics is a growing issue in our society (DeWitt-Heffner & Oxenford, 2001). DeWitt-Heffner and Oxenford noted three types of cyberethics issues have emerged online: intellectual property, privacy/security, and free speech/hate speech (p. 101). Intellectual property issues include plagiarism of other's people work and ideas, software pirating, and illegal downloading and sharing of music and movies. Hacking falls under privacy and security issues, and free speech/hate issues abound on the Internet, with people posting more and more blogs and videos with little or no censoring (DeWitt-Heffner & Oxenford, 2001). At every turn, students (and adults) are faced with multiple ethical dilemmas each time they get online.

Corporate scandals are filled with ethical misbehavior. Companies like Enron, Tyco, and WorldCom have become household names. Unfortunately, the media attention garnered by these companies also has made it easier for students to justify their own actions.

In 2002, the Josephson Institute conducted a survey about cheating, lying, and stealing among high school students. More than 12,000 students were surveyed. Among those students, first-time exam cheating had risen from 61% in 1992 to 74% in 2002. The number of respondents reporting lying to teachers also had increased from 69% to 83%.

Electronic tools that make writing easier, such as cutting and pasting, also have made it easier for students to falsify and plagiarize documents. "Cut-and-paste plagiarism" has put a new spin on taking exams. It has turned English teachers into detectives and taken time away from teaching (Winter, Winter, & Emerson, 2003). At the collegiate level, students have hacked into textbook publisher Web sites, found sample exams, and shared them with their peers (McCabe, Trevino, & Butterfield, 2001).

"Virtual world" dilemmas are nothing new for today's students. All students face these questions at one time or another. The difference, however, is in the way they respond to these situations. Is persistence considered stalking? Is it OK to "spoof" someone, or pretend you are someone else? How can there be consequences for something done in fun?

The Internet and its freedom—good or bad—places the responsibility in the hands of the user. Empowering students to make decisions that have a positive impact on their future is the responsibility of parents and teachers, and students have to learn there are consequences for their actions—even those conducted online while no one else is watching.

Students cheat for a number of reasons. Some cheat because they fear failure; others, because they fear disappointing parents due to low school performance (Lathrop & Foss, 2000). Teaching right from wrong isn't always easy—or completely black and white. Today's students are on the go. Like adults, they need all the shortcuts they can get. They face deadlines for school assignments, are involved in extracurricular activities, and may hold a part-time job—all potential reasons for students to rationalize unethical behavior online.

Technology has provided many opportunities to help meet the demands facing today's busy students. It also has provided an additional way to cut corners on assignments and tests. In fact, at least 10% of students admit to plagiarizing information found on the Internet (Valenza, 2003–2004). When it comes to online behavior, there are many gray areas. Technology has changed the way exams are taken and assignments are completed, and there is a greater tolerance than ever before. Once unacceptable behaviors are now pervasive in the culture (Lathrop & Foss, 2005). Students are using technology such as calculators, cell phones, PDAs, pagers, and iPods to cheat in school (Popyack et al., 2003).

In her book, *I Found It on the Internet: Coming of Age Online*, Francis Jacobson Harris provides insight into the online world of teenagers. Because today's teenagers have never known a time without computers, they are always connected. Technology has created a fine line between school and socializing—one often seems to spill over into the other. Researching has become collaborative. Students ask questions about other students' work while doing their own project. At the same time, they may advise another friend about their topic and how they plan to do it (Jacobson-Harris, 2005).

Collaboration and sharing information seem to go hand-in-hand. Some students are preoccupied with locating the information, rather than questioning its source. For some, screening the information is a problem. Teachers report that students have difficulty recognizing that the author's work is his or her own, and that the work should be credited to that person, even if the student is rephrasing the idea (Jacobson-Harris, 2005). Many teens are under the impression that authored articles were developed for their benefit, and some students follow the rules only when they know it is in their best interest to do so. This "WIIFM Principle" (what is in it for me) often sets the standard for students' online behavior (Johnson, 2003).

In a study on academic dishonesty, researchers discovered students had their own perceptions about cheating. According to one student,

> I believe there are two kinds of cheating—one is bad and real cheating, whereas the other is not really cheating, or acceptable cheating, something we all do. Bad cheating is when you try to cheat off the

person sitting next to you, maybe a friend, without him seeing or knowing about it. However, when you have a hard exam on a very long subject, you are likely to be confused and need some help. You can ask your friend who is sitting in front of you, and he can either tell you or refuse to answer you back, so you won't be forcing him to do anything. (Popyack et al., 2003, p. 48)

Cheating has become a way of life where, unfortunately, crime often does pay and cheaters are seldom caught or punished (Lathrop & Foss, 2005). In most cases, schools still expect students to adhere to the rules regarding cheating, but some changes are taking place. Some schools are allowing students to use the Internet during tests, search online Cliffs Notes, and use their handhelds to compare answers on science drills. These changes are definitely spurring debate among educators (Gamerman, 2006). The world of high-tech cheating has schools, teachers, and parents wondering how to deal with the issue.

Frank Levy, professor of Urban Economics at MIT, believes that failing to teach students how to navigate the knowledge economy is like putting them on a track without the train (Gamerman, 2006). In some cases, neuroscientists believe there may be a reason for this misbehavior. The teenage brain is unlike those of their parents and teachers. It does not allow them to function in the same way and their perception of an event can be very different. In fact, MRIs indicate that teens make many decisions from a part of their brain that is still developing. This can lead to a problem in perception. Impulse rules over reason, and the tendency to "push the envelope," whether in sports, behind the wheel, or at the computer, can leave adults stunned by students' actions and lead to strained communications.

Computer-savvy kids face additional challenges. Many of them find it difficult to acknowledge that what they are doing is wrong—and may, in fact, not view it as unethical. Security measures taken by the school only make them feel they cannot be trusted (Jacobson-Harris, 2005).

Potential Solutions

Many schools and educators are looking for solutions to this expanding problem of using technology to cheat in the classroom. Turnitin (http://www.turnitin.com), a Web-based program, was created when John M. Barrie, a graduate of the University of Berkeley, was asked to do something about the growing number of cheaters. In response, he created Turnitin software to identify plagiarized passages of text (Glod, 2006).

The system checks student work in a database of more than 60 million papers and essays. It also cross-references more than 12 billion Web sources and 10,000 online newspapers, magazines, and journals. On completion, each student receives an "originality report" for his or her work. However, programs like these tend to be costly, and that kind of bill can be outrageous when dealing with a large school system (Glod, 2006).

In addition to Turnitin, a number of other tools are available to detect plagiarism. Educators and schools should spend time researching which is the best fit with their particular district and needs. These include, but are not limited to:

- JPlag (software plagiarism; https://www.ipd.uni-karlsruhe.de/jplag)
- EVE2 (http://www.canexus.com/eve/index.shtml)
- Moss (http://theory.stanford.edu/~aiken/moss)
- WCopyfind (The Plagiarism Resource Site; http://plagiarism.phys.virginia.edu)

Character development is yet another means of introducing ethical behavior to students in the classroom. Such decision-making begins at an early age. Once children have reached middle school, their values have been ingrained (Titus, 1994). Attitudes regarding ethics, good and bad, have developed, thus the best time to introduce these skills is when a child is in elementary school.

Muriel Summers, principal of A.B. Combs Leadership Magnet Elementary School in Raleigh, NC, incorporated character development into the school's K–5 curriculum. Once a month, Summers meets with the students and gives them a chance to voice their concerns, making them change agents in their own school. They soon learn their input makes a difference.

Key to its success is its approach. More than reading about an historical figure or spending time addressing responsibility, students are given real-life examples of the pros and cons of actions they may be considering. Before long, they discover why certain behaviors are not appropriate. They also come to understand they may face some kind of a consequence for their actions. She shared a story about a student who was caught text messaging during a test. His reasons, thought legitimate, were not acceptable. "It all boils down to making good and bad choices and what happens when you don't" noted Summers (M. Summers, personal communication, April 2007).

Teaching good decision making is more than just a lesson. It can have far-reaching effects into the child's future, influencing the way he or she responds to conflict, perseveres, and takes risks. Knowing how to think about choices ahead of time can make a difference in the ethical decisions students will make when they are older. Summers summed it up when she said, "Character education is the celebration of children that make great choices" (M. Summers, personal communication, April 2007).

Increasing Teacher Awareness

Popyack et al. (2003) discovered teachers were not always aware of how their students were cheating. They ask, "Did you know . . .":

1. cell phones can be used to text message answers to other classmates?
2. forgetting to "log out" when leaving a class provides a perfect opportunity for other students to use that student's account and identity?
3. electronic paper mills advise students on how to use their services?
4. students can outsource assignments by hiring someone to do small projects for them?
5. Web sites will find someone to help students with their homework for a fee?
6. students can receive help through e-mail solicitations?
7. cell phones with Web browsers will allow students to look up answers while taking an exam? (Argetsinger, 2003)
8. expert help in any subject is available through http:// allexperts.com?

Schwartau (2001) listed a number of decisions that compromise student integrity. Students should be aware that these behaviors are unethical and are not acceptable online behavior:

1. Using cell phones to get even with other classmates.
2. Breaking into someone else's computer as a "joke" or for revenge.
3. Editing digital pictures of someone without their permission.
4. Spreading rumors about friends or teachers online because it can be done anonymously.

5. Stalking someone because they "broke off" the relationship.
6. Sending unwanted phone calls to a random number just to harass them.
7. Creating a phony Web site to gain popularity with someone or another group.
8. Cutting and pasting from various sources to complete an assignment and call it your own.
9. Sending e-mail attachments that will infect someone else's computer.

Unethical behavior is a daily occurrence online. It takes place at home, school, or anywhere that provides a hot spot for computer access. Each day, students and adults are faced with decisions that could influence their grades, compromise their work, or affect their relationships. Teachers should be aware that new technologies have offered a wide range of opportunities for students to use the computer in ways that may be unethical or allow them to cheat.

Cyberethics is about two things: right and wrong. It has to do with values and ethics and how to behave online. Opportunities regarding hacking, cheating, and the use of papermills for term papers have become widespread. Internet usage is universal, but it also comes with a responsibility to the user. Students are empowered by the ways the computer can alter, improve, and manipulate information. Teaching them how to become better "digital citizens" is part of that responsibility.

It is not always easy to get caught online, but it is up to the teacher to bring some of these issues to the forefront. Be prepared to have students discuss issues like cutting and pasting, using technology to cheat on tests, spreading viruses, or posting untruths about their peers. Allow them to discuss these issues among themselves, or set up a blog to explore these issues further.

Cyberethics is about making the correct choices. It is a personal responsibility. Thinking about one's actions is the best way to teach digital citizenship and the role students play each time they are online.

Online Technologies: Playgrounds for Tech-Savvy Kids

"In order to do things differently, you have to see things differently."

—Paul Allaire, former CEO, Xerox Corporation

NEW technology buzzwords are being heard every day. *Folksonomies, tagging, RSS,* and *collective intelligence* are just a few terms used to describe exciting changes that are taking place on the Internet. These tools allow people to collaborate and share information online. Unlike the Internet of the past, which was mainly used to shop, check e-mail, or do research, these tools allow us to use the Internet to connect with others, seek help, and provide opinions on topics of interest. Best of all, these tools, among others, are free.

These new Web tools provide options for tech-savvy kids to demonstrate their know-how. It provides a hands-on approach to using text, pictures, audio, and video. Collaboration is learned early on as students share information and construct original ideas. Blogging, wikis, podcasting, social bookmarking, and geocaching, among others, all are tools that students easily adapt to—and ones that prepare them for work in today's global market.

Social networking sites have been gaining in popularity for some time. Today, MySpace has more than 65 million members, and Flickr, which allows photo sharing and other multimedia services, has more than 2.5 million (Levy & Stone, 2006). Both sites continue to grow exponentially. There is debate as to whether or not these social networking sites should be permitted in schools. Students need to be trained how to use these tools in an acceptable way, both at school and at home. There is concern that students give out too much information over sites like MySpace and Facebook and that they could face danger. Educators should go over the various privacy settings for such sites with students, deliberately pointing out which information is inappropriate to include on profiles. Schools and libraries receiving funding often are directed to ban student use of these sites on school premises (O'Hear, 2006). Nevertheless, even when this occurs, teaching students how to use these tools in a safe and ethical manner is necessary (see Chapters 1 and 2).

Technology as a Form of Differentiation

Technology can be used to differentiate content for all students. Gifted students need opportunities to experience greater depth and breadth of the content being taught, and technology is one way to help differentiate. There are certain strategies that can benefit students who are tech-savvy and looking for new ways to express ideas. Among these are learning contracts, telementoring opportunities, online clustered groups, and independent projects.

Technology also has provided students with a means to motivate their learning. New Web tools continue to be available that make students more eager than ever to use them in assignments. These students usually are able to self-pace through content on their own, make decisions regarding an assignment, and arrive at a decision based on their findings. Providing them with the most up-to-date strategies to use in their assignments can make the classroom an exciting place to express what many already know.

How can I incorporate technology as a form of differentiation in my classroom?

1. Allow students to integrate technology into their assignments according to depth and interest. Allow students to negotiate independent projects. Use a learning contract to outline the process.
2. Technology can assist students in self-pacing through assignments, making it easier for them to complete the coursework at their own speed.
3. Have students collaborate on writing projects, community service projects, or projects that connect student globally, using technology applications.
4. Scaffold various technology strategies to create new and more complex products (e.g., documentaries, visual essays, etc.).
5. Give students the opportunity to explore other educational opportunities that incorporate technology, such as virtual schools and distance learning.

Technology Ideas for the Classroom

Technology is now at everyone's fingertips, and as more and more schools and classrooms gain online access, many exciting tools are available for teachers to incorporate into their daily lessons. Information on some of the most popular tools is included below. Each technology is defined, and ideas for using it in the classroom are provided.

Folksonomies

A *folksonomy* can be thought of as a way to categorize information on the Internet, similar to how books are catalogued in the library using the Dewey Decimal System. This has become increasingly popular in the past few years, as users are able to classify information and share it with others. In order to categorize information, tags must be assigned to the content. For example, on Flickr, a photo-sharing Web site (http://www.flickr.com), users are able to post their photos and include descriptive tags, which allow them to be categorized using those terms. When other users on that Web site do a search for "computer," for example, all of the pictures with that descriptive tag will pop up (almost 550,000 at the time of publication). In addition, sites like del.icio.us (http://delicious.com) and Technorati (http://www.technorati.com) are driven by folksonomies, but in these two cases users bookmark Web sites and blogs, respectively, to share with others.

Flickr can be incorporated in the classroom, and is easily adapted for different grade levels and subjects. Students can be charged with the task of using five Flickr images to create a visual narrative. By using Flickr's tag cloud, or searchable database of photo titles, students can find user-submitted images and juxtapose seemingly dissimilar images together into one stream to tell a story.

Big Huge Labs (http://bighugelabs.com/flickr) identifies creative things students can do with digital photographs. The tools on this site are designed to be compatible with Flickr. Students can create their own badges, calendars, posters, magazine covers, and more.

The Flickr world map function (http://www.flickr.com/map) is very useful to middle and high school geography or history teachers, as it can be used to help students illustrate key points of a battle or other historical event through images. In addition, it could be used in an elementary school classroom as a way for students to show classmates their summer vacation route. The applications are truly only limited by the teacher's—and the students'—creativity.

How can I use folksonomies in the classroom?

1. Have students take photos with digital cameras, upload the pictures to a site like Flickr, and then determine which tags to include with their photos and how they should be categorized. Photos can be taken to demonstrate a new concept learned (e.g., various geometry shapes from around the school) and shared with the rest of the class by using specific tags.

2. When conducting research online, have students use tagging function to tag important Web sites that they find helpful. Unlike bookmarking favorite Web sites on one computer, students are able to retrieve these tagged sites on any browser, thus making it easier to access Web pages they've found to be helpful.

3. Have students incorporate sites like Big Huge Labs with pictures from Flickr to create movie-style posters to recall certain historical events or billboards to demonstrate pros and cons of controversial issues.

4. Share information with your students by tagging specific Web sites, blogs, and articles online that relate to the lesson being taught and having students access these pages to view the material.

RSS

RSS stands for Really Simple Syndication (Stamatiou, 2005). An RSS feed is something that a user subscribes to in order to be notified when new content has been posted on a Web site. Instead of visiting multiple Web sites to see whether new information, such as an article or blog entry, has been added to a site, a user can go to one RSS feed reader site and view the latest RSS feeds from multiple Web sites. This is an easy way to determine whether a Web site has been updated, and it allows the user to get a quick preview of what has been added by showing the title and usually a brief sample of the content. You will notice a small (often orange) RSS icon on Web sites in which an RSS feed is available (Stamatiou, 2005).

One of the most popular RSS readers (or aggregators) is Bloglines (http://www.bloglines.com). Bloglines is an ideal application for the classroom and can be used for dual purposes. The RSS reader provides a forum for real-time journaling, self-expression, and a platform for improving vocabulary, proving to be an effective tool for teaching students. At the same time, a blog is a positive way to promote parent and student interaction. Blog accounts allow teachers to communicate with parents, keeping them up to date on homework assignments and school news, and opening a dialogue for busy parents to stay in touch with what is happening in their child's classroom. An RSS reader helps parents and students know when new information has been posted, therefore keeping them updated in a timely manner.

How can I use RSS in the classroom?

1. Write a blog (see Blog section for more information) to keep parents and students abreast of what is happening in your classroom, such as homework and upcoming functions, and have readers subscribe to the RSS feed to be updated when you have posted new information.

2. If your students have blogs, use an RSS reader to subscribe to them. You will be notified as soon as their blogs have been updated, thus allowing you to skim over what they've written in a short amount of time. If you'd like to make comments on their work, you can click on the entry and be taken to their site.

3. Have students set up accounts on Bloglines when doing research. Students can identify specific topics that will help them as they conduct research, and will be notified as soon as new information on these topics has been added to Web sites. This is a great way to keep them interested in, and knowledgeable about, current events in a timely manner.

4. Have students use an RSS reader to compare information on a specific topic. They can look at three–four different sources and compare and contrast the information found in each. This is a great way to help teach students how to know whether a source is valid.

Social Networking Sites

For parents and educators alike, social networking sites like MySpace and Facebook are double-edged swords. Most social networking sites support the maintenance of preexisting social networks, but others help strangers connect based on shared interests, political views, or activities. Some sites cater to diverse audiences, while others attract people based on common language or shared racial, sexual, religious, or nationality-based identities. Sites also vary in the extent to which they incorporate new information and communication tools, such as mobile connectivity, blogging, and photo/video sharing.

Koterwas (2007) noted that the National School Boards Association believes "that safety concerns over online social networking are overblown, and recommends that schools become more comfortable with social networks and seek educational uses for online social networking" (para. 1). About 52% of school districts have banned access to social networking sites. Although some parents and educators are concerned about the safety of social networking sites—which can expose students not only to unfamiliar adults, but also to numerous advertising and commercial images—educators can integrate safe social networking into their curricula. Social networking sites are on the increase for young children, and include sites like Imbee (http://www.imbee.com), Club Penguin (http://www.clubpenguin.com), Whyville (http:// www.whyville.net), and Webkinz (http://www.webkinz.com). However, participation in these Web communities sometimes requires a membership fee or purchase of a product, making it difficult to incorporate in the classroom.

ePals (http://www.epals.com) is a successful program for elementary through high school students. It connects students from one location to another, allowing children from a small town in Nebraska to connect with students on the other side of the world. ePals allows schools and teachers to share ideas at the global level, while students are introduced to foreign languages and new cultures through a Web-based community.

How can I use (or address) social networking sites in my classroom?

1. Have students work collaboratively with peers to do research. For older students, opensource software, like Google docs can be a positive choice.

2. Create an awareness campaign. Have students create brochures and a plan to educate parents and teachers about how social networking is being used in schools and libraries. They should investigate how their own school deals with these issues.

3. Use a wiki format to debate any local, national and state legislation that plans to regulate social networking sites.

4. Produce a podcast as a way to teach educators, parents, and the community about social networking and the possibilities beyond Facebook.

5. Host a Technology Day where teens learn how to use Flickr, del.icio.us, My Space, and Technorati. Ethical issues also can be addressed. (Young Adult Library Services Association, n.d.).

Blogs

Blogs (short for Web logs) are diaries of the 21st century, created and read solely online, that include links and other Web-based materials. It is a great way to share introspective ideas, to vent, and to identify with others. Blogs can range from a simple three-word post to a full commentary about a particular subject. According to Siegle (2007), "blogs promote interaction among individuals while maintaining a text record of the free flow of ideas" (p. 19). They also can include links to other Web pages and blogs. There are a variety of media used in blogging, including video (videoblogs), photographs (photoblogs), and audio (podcasting; Richardson, 2006).

In its best form, blogging is a reflection. For students who like to write and engage others in debate, it also can be very powerful. Best of all, blogs can be fun, motivational, and creative. They can be used to address real-world problems where all voices can be heard regardless of their point of view. Students can begin at the local level, usually in their own class and, under a teacher's guidance, connect with others at a global level. The Presidential race, the environment, and stem cell research are all topics, sometimes controversial, that may interest gifted students. Student opinions on topics similar to these can be very strong, along with their wish to express them. Exposing them to societal issues is a great way to learn how others perceive current events, and blogs are one way to put forth ideas for others to read.

Students need to be taught how to blog. They need to learn how to stay on the subject they are discussing, while making appropriate comments on other people's blogs at the same time. Blogs are a great way to have students work on their writing skills—in a fun and exciting manner. It is important for student bloggers to demonstrate respect for other people's viewpoints. Students need to understand that personal attacks on others are not acceptable and will not be tolerated.

Blogging is not just for older students. Elementary students can use blogs to post, write about, and discuss topics. Nancy Bosch's third-grade gifted class blogged about black holes, the theory of relativity, "50 Things I Would Not Be Caught Dead Wearing," and talent shows. They caught on fast, and the only frustration was the lack of time available to work on the blogs for extended periods of time.

During an election year, a high school English teacher and history teacher collaborated to create a project that would help students understand about the voting process. The school was in the process of choosing a student body president. Much like a real presidential election, the teachers believed the best way to encourage student participation in the election was through a vote, and determined that candidates and voters could share their thoughts and opinions using blogs. Grades 9–12 would take part in the school's "First Presidential Blog." It was a way to involve everyone and if it went well, the school could repeat it in the next student body presidential election.

Candidates had their own blog with which they could share their platform, and the only requirement was to "think about what they were writing." Each student was required to adhere to ethical conduct: It was not a platform for pranks. Although not everyone was familiar with blogging, the project was a fun motivator and many students participated.

One type of blog that is relevant in the science classroom is an environmental blog. Environmental blogs are ways to introduce students to issues and online communities that are passionate about the Earth. Environmental bloggers are willing to engage in any "green" topic. Connecting passionate students with each other can provide new perspectives on topics and introduce them to different ways of thinking. The blog can be used as a dialogue to address local issues, such as protecting open space, wildlife habitat, coastal changes, or the piping plover. Although each city and state will have individual needs, this is a good way to let students interact and brainstorm ideas to improve the situation at the same time.

A forerunner to the blog was the online journal, which is an excellent option for the elementary teacher who wishes to lay the groundwork for blogging. Online journals allow students to take part in their own learning, take the time to consider ideas, and learn how to express them. They generally are less public than blogs and contain fewer links and other embedded material. There are a number of ways these journals can be used. Dialogue journals are conversations in writing that allow students to learn the importance of expressing themselves. They usually take place between a student and teacher, and the topic most often is related to a subject specific to an assignment or topic of study. In this exercise, students learn how to communicate informally and may start to think how their responses sound to others. An online version of the dialogue journal enables students to get used to the technology and provides great practice for writing a future blog.

Online math journals take the concept of math one step further, as students are asked to express their understanding of the problems they solve in writing. Through this practice, students who leap from the problem's beginning to the answer are forced to revisit the way they arrived at a solution. (However, gifted math students may find this approach frustrating if they just "know" the answer.)

Online science journals encourage students to think like a scientist as they conduct their own experiments and research. Pondering the experiment also helps the students learn how to express their own ideas and opinions.

There are many benefits to online journals. They help solve problems and encourage students to reflect on their ideas. They allow students to learn from one another by sharing thoughts, experiences, and opinions. These journals also help the teacher recognize anxieties, personal issues, and what motivates the student's behavior.

Tech-savvy bloggers may see things differently from other students. Connecting them with peers who also have strong opinions can make a dialogue on a topic energizing and motivating for those who participate. When students come across peers with convictions different from their own, it can force them to evaluate both viewpoints.

How can I use blogs in my classroom?

1. Use blogging to integrate a writing or literature assignment. Allow students to express their thoughts about the book and discuss the author's intent for writing it.

2. Have students address local concerns by maintaining a school blog focused on making a difference in the community.

3. Plan virtual field trips to places like coral reefs or Woods Hole Oceanographic Institution to study coastal ecology. Have students use their findings to blog about solutions and ideas to "green" challenges.

4. Use blogs to set up a cultural exchange between students from different countries in which students discuss their daily lives and comment on other blog entries. Blogging can be used a means to understand each other's perspective on other cultures while helping students to reveal their own feelings.

5. Use blogs to introduce students to tolerance and the acceptance of new ideas.

Forums

Forums are part of an online community that allows students to exchange ideas and helps them become more responsive to what their peers have to say (Christopher, Thomas, & Tallent-Runnels, 2004). This communication takes place through e-mail, instant messaging, and chat. Forums can be issue oriented and allow participants to express different viewpoints and take part in debates. Online forums promote higher level thinking skills and create connections for students by helping them analyze and apply new knowledge. Postings make it easy to know which topics pertain to individual interests.

Christopher et al. (2004) used a rubric to encourage graduate-level gifted students to use higher level thinking skill when posting to an online discussion (see Table 1). This rubric could be used for students taking part in forums that address content, controversial issues, and other course requirements in both elementary and secondary schools.

How can I use forums in my classroom?

1. Use forums to have students explore various types of literature and exchange ideas.

2. Have students post questions about subjects they are studying and respond to each other.

3. Use forums as a way to get everyone to voice an opinion on a topic. Some students may not feel comfortable contributing to an oral discussion in class. However, these same students may be the ones who are able to make profound comments in an online discussion.

4. Use forums to let students respond to controversial topics.

5. Let students use the forum to discuss their own personal topics of interest. This is a good way for students to share their interests with their classmates, and allows people with similar interests to hold an online discussion about their passion.

Podcasting

A group of sixth graders from a school in Kansas were huddled around their computers, preparing a podcast for a school in Guatemala. The cultural exchange allowed them to learn about the language and the customs in Guatemala. Each student had his or her own blog and the class had its own Web site, but with the addition of podcasting, the exchange connected all of them in a more personal manner.

"In its simplest form, a podcast is a digitalized audio file that is stored on the Internet and can be downloaded and played on listeners' computers or MP3 players" (Siegle, 2007, p. 14). Most browsers allow users to play podcasts using media file players, and both Apple (iTunes for both Mac and Windows platforms; http://www.apple.com/itunes/download) and Microsoft (Windows Media Player; http://www.microsoft.com/windows/

Table 1

Rubric for Evaluation of Online Discussion Prompts and Response

Levels of Thinking	Points	Process Verbs	Behavior Descriptors
Low: Remember or Understand	1	explain, list, describe, recall, define, identify, show, restate, summarize, list, demonstrate, illustrate, explain	Behaviors that emphasize, recall a memory, or indicate a literal understanding
Medium: Apply or Analyze	2	organize, classify, relate, prioritize, discuss, group, model, apply, compare, contrast, distinguish, categorize, take apart, combine	Behaviors that require students to use what they have learned in a new way or that break down knowledge into its component parts
High: Evaluate or Create	3	extend, design, reconstruct, reorganize, create, develop, speculate, propose, predict, generate, interpret, judge, justify, critique, evaluate, use criteria, dispute	Behaviors that combine learning into a new whole or that assess the value of particular ideas or solutions

Note. From "Raising the Bar: Encouraging High Level Thinking in Online Discussion Forums," by M. M. Christopher, J. A. Thomas, and M. L. Tallent-Runnels, 2004, *Roeper Review, 26.* Copyright © 2004 by *Roeper Review.* Reprinted with permission of author.

windowsmedia/player/default.aspx) provide free media players for download (Siegle, 2007).

Podcasts can be played at any time, making them an ideal medium for the classroom. Foreign language teachers can record and publish daily practice sessions. Social studies teachers can use them in oral histories and interviews, and music teachers can use them to record special music for their students to hear (Richardson, 2006). Individual music teachers also can use them to provide practice clips so the student knows how a piece of music should sound before they begin learning it. For a variety of podcasts on various topics, educators can visit the Education Podcast Network (http:///www.epnweb.org; Siegle, 2007). In addition, the Teacher's Podcast (http://www.teacherspodcast.org) was created by Kathy King and Mark Gura to provide a place for teachers to become part of a listening community. The site already has more than 130 hours of podcasts with no indication of slowing down.

Creating a podcast is inexpensive and most kids (and teachers!) catch on in no time. Podcasting can be used in a variety of ways. It can be used to record interviews or share information. It can be used to broadcast a hot debate or as a forum to expand a science experiment. Musicians and rising actors also find podcasts a great way to express their talent.

For young children, podcasting can help them learn about new topics. They are able to share what they know with others as they learn how to use the technology. Book reviews are a positive way to introduce this concept to young children. Even 5-year-olds can tell you about a book they read—with the added excitement of hearing their own voice. This tool makes it easy to share book reports with parents remotely, and teachers can showcase students' work on their class Web site.

Podcasts turn students into creators rather than consumers. The technology teaches them how to produce information—rather than merely watching the events as they take place around them. They learn how to focus their ideas through practice, and soon realize their ideas can reach a much larger audience through the use of this technology. Moreover, podcasting goes way beyond individualization, teaching students how to work in teams and collaborate with others in various locations, both locally and internationally.

Creating a Podcast. Having students create their own podcasts can be exciting and an addition to the technology tools you can use with them in the classroom. With schools facing a multitude of budget considerations, podcasts are an easy and expensive way to incorporate technology. Classrooms will need access to a computer with a microphone and Internet access. Flanagan and Calandra (2005) outlined four basic steps to creating a podcast:

- Use an audio editing program to record your podcast.
- Upload your podcast in MP3 format to a Web server, taking note of the podcast's URL.
- Create a blog and insert the podcast's URL.
- Convert your blog URL into an RSS feed and share this with others who may be interested in your podcast. (p. 22)

Audacity (http://audacity.sourceforge.net) is a free, easy-to-use editing program recommended for most podcasters, as it is for Mac, Windows, or Linux platforms (Flanagan & Calandra, 2005; Siegle, 2007). Students can record themselves talking and then edit their recording using this program. Audacity features many audio effects that students may enjoy trying as they edit their recordings. Audacity allows users to save their audio recording in MP3 format, which can then be played on any computer or MP3 player. As Flanagan and Calandra suggested, users may want to create a blog or Web site that features their podcast and then upload the podcast to it. For those who are more advanced and would like to share the podcast with others using an RSS feed, one free Web site to help do so is PodCastBlaster (http://www.podcastblaster.com; Siegle, 2007).

> **How can I use podcasting in my classroom?**
> 1. Use a podcast to provide an overview of the day's lesson, meeting the needs of a number of different learning styles. Downloading this gives students immediate access and keeps all students informed of assignments.
> 2. Have students do research on a topic, develop scripts, and then prepare podcasts to teach others what they've learned.
> 3. Have your students use the podcast to broadcast information on special news events like the spelling bee, Destination Imagination, or band concerts. Use them to create commercials about upcoming dances or sports events and as a way to interview coaches, teachers, and team athletes.
> 4. Introduce potential theatre students to fine arts podcasts and video lessons on iTunes U (http://www.apple.com/education/itunesu_mobilelearning/itunesu.html) where they can learn what to expect as they get closer to the next musical, theatrical, or dance audition.
> 5. Have art students work with an art museum to create a series of podcasts on a group of artists as a way to understand the paintings. Students also can develop a tour of the museum from their viewpoint to keep as a resource for other art classes.

WebQuests

Every classroom contains students who have questions and curiosity that go beyond the lesson. Meeting that need can be a challenge for even the most creative teacher. These self-directed students with enthusiasm for learning can find themselves immersed in topics that open up a new perspective on the lesson at hand. Students need an activity that will engage them in the classroom while opening up unknown topics of interest at the same time.

The WebQuest model was created by Dr. Bernie Dodge in 1995. Defined as "an inquiry-oriented lesson format in which most or all the information that learners work with comes from the Web," WebQuests are a positive learning tool for students ("What Is a WebQuest?", n.d.). They provide students with real-world problems, require higher level thinking skills, and can be used individually or in a group. These activities allow students to work at their own pace. Not only do students get to learn more about the topic of focus, they get to experience it in greater depth than found in the typical curriculum as they pace their way through the WebQuest, discovering something new at every link.

There are a number of collections available to teachers new to WebQuests. They can be a starting point or a springboard to creating your own. WebQuest.org lists more than 2,500 Web-Quests that have been developed by teachers in school districts and universities. They are updated on a regular basis and provide a resource of topics ranging from art, to English, to math, to science, to life skills for grades K–12 and even adults. In addition, BestWebQuests.com (http://bestwebquests.com) contains numerous WebQuests by content areas and grade level, and ranks them using specific criteria.

According to WebQuest.org, a WebQuest is defined by the following attributes. A WebQuest:

- is wrapped around a doable and interesting task that is ideally a scaled down version of things that adults do as citizens or workers;
- requires higher level thinking, not simply summarizing;
- makes good use of the Web;

- isn't a research report or a step-by-step science or math procedure; and
- isn't just a series of Web-based experiences. ("Creating Web-Quests," n.d., para. 2)

In a WebQuest, students cannot just click a link and visit a Web page—and be finished! WebQuests are much more in depth and focus on higher level thinking. First, teachers must select a topic that engages students in higher level thinking skills. These topics can be developed with certain students in mind, especially those who demonstrate an understanding of technology. The topics most likely will align somehow with the curriculum being taught, but allow for a more in-depth view of one aspect of it. WebQuests can be aligned with state or national standards to ensure that students are learning and using the desired skills.

For novice WebQuest writers, templates were created to make the design process easier and a number of these are available to teachers. These online authoring programs are available at no cost. Filamentality (http://www.kn.pacbell.com/wired/fil) is a fill-in-the-blank tool that guides you through the process of creating a WebQuest. It helps you pick a topic, locate links on the Internet, and then develop activities to go along with what you've found. zWebQuest (http://www.zunal.com) is a Web-based software that provides an online tutorial for creating WebQuests. Finally, PHP WebQuest (http://eduforge.org/projects/phpwebquest) generates WebQuests for teachers and allows images to be uploaded and resized as needed.

For those wanting to develop their own version, Schweizer and Kossow (2007) outlined the five critical components (or some variation of) found in most WebQuests:
- Introduction,
- Task (or Problem),

- Process,
- Evaluation, and
- Conclusion.

The *Introduction* is used to introduce the topic at hand. This is usually written in a way to get students intrigued in the WebQuest and to create an interest in learning more about the topic. The *Task* (or *Problem*) exposes students "to a specific, open-ended activity and their role in that activity is discussed" (Schweizer & Kossow, 2007, p. 31). This component briefly outlines what the students' task will be in a clear and concise manner. This leads to the *Process* section, in which students find the steps they must complete for the WebQuest. The assessment criteria and expectations for the final product created by the student are included in the Process (Schweizer & Kossow, 2007). In addition, some teachers include the hyperlinks that students must visit in this section (although others may put it in a separate section of the WebQuest). The *Evaluation* is usually in the form of a rubric, which contains the criteria by which students will be evaluated. Many WebQuests employ self-evaluation tools in which students evaluate their own performance and quality of work. Finally, the *Conclusion* ties the project together. It tends to reiterate what students should have learned and completed during the WebQuest, and often includes additional information and links for students who are interested in learning more about the topic.

Depending on the topic, you may want to design a questionnaire for your students ahead of time to see what they would like included in the WebQuest. This will make them part of the process and make the topic more interesting. You also may want to send them on their own quest to find links to use in the project. It will be a good opportunity to discuss and evaluate links.

This student-centered approach will have them wanting to create their own WebQuests that they can share with classmates. Designing their own WebQuests teaches them how to question what they are learning.

How can I use WebQuests in my classroom?

1. Develop a WebQuest to cover a topic you will be teaching. This can get students interested in learning more about the topic, as well as become an advanced organizer.

2. Ask students to develop a WebQuest for a topic that has just been taught in class. Allow them to come up with their own ideas, negotiate their own product and timeline, and sign a learning contract pertaining to a product associated with the WebQuest.

3. Have the students create WebQuests for other classes to complete. They can define problems, devise solutions, and exercise higher level thinking skills by creating their own WebQuests. This helps them expand their own thinking while meeting the needs of others at the same time.

4. Have students get involved in their own community by connecting them to real-world events (e.g., the election, the environment, or the town council). Download related WebQuests and use them as a point of discussion and information for current topics.

5. For students interested in art, use them as a way to introduce different time periods and artists. WebQuests can be used for music students to introduce them to different composers, music, and eras. They also can be used as a starting point for students focusing on future careers.

e-Portfolios

An electronic portfolio (*e-portfolio*) is a group of text, graphics, audio, and video artifacts that show the student's learning and growth during his or her school years. It demonstrates a student's abilities and achievements in more than one area, providing fluid examples of achievement as a student progresses through school. Portrayed through artwork, writing samples, and teacher recommendations, among other items, the e-portfolio is a way for students to share their achievement with family, teachers, and peers. It also is a tool to share with potential colleges and employers.

Electronic portfolios are student-centered and are created with the student in mind. They empower students to share their work with others by demonstrating success and growth in their strongest subjects and outside activities. The e-portfolio becomes a digital history and story of the student's life. It is told through a history of coursework taken, narratives, artwork, musical pieces, or any activity that demonstrates the student's involvement.

Teachers also can display their growth through e-portfolios According to Barrett (2002), both teachers and students develop the following life-long learning skills through the creation process of e-portfolios:

- *Collection*: Teachers and students learn to save artifacts that represent the successes (and "growth opportunities") in their day-to-day teaching and learning.
- *Selection*: Teachers and students review and evaluate the artifacts they have saved, and identify those that demonstrate achievement of specific standards (this is where most electronic portfolios stop).
- *Reflection*: Teachers and students become reflective practitioners, evaluating their own growth over time and their achievement of the standards, as well as the gaps in their development.
- *Projection*: Teachers and students compare their reflections to the standards and performance indicators, and set learn-

ing goals for the future. This is the stage that turns portfolio development into professional development and supports lifelong learning.

- *Presentation*: Teachers and students share their portfolios with their peers. This is the stage where appropriate "public" commitments can be made to encourage collaboration and commitment to professional development and lifelong learning. (p. 3)

Student-centered e-portfolios can be a creative way to convey students' learning and accomplishments each year. Empowering students to take part in their future can be strengthened by use of the e-portfolio. Ideas to keep in mind when students develop their e-portfolio:

- Encourage students to select their best work over the course of the year.
- Encourage students to include a variety of samples (i.e., writing, artwork, recommendations, narratives, performance clips).
- Allow tech-savvy kids to use as many Web tools as possible to create their e-portfolio.

Because the process of creating the portfolio is equally important, some schools have chosen to include a presentation component. This will allow the student to present his or her updates on a yearly basis and reflect on what he or she has accomplished, as well as future goals.

The e-portfolio will need a place to be stored. Some schools may allow the e-portfolios to be saved to the district server, although limited people usually have access to the server, thus making it difficult to share the portfolio with others (Siegle, 2002a). Other options include having students save their work on CD-ROMs (which are limited in space), DVDs, or Web sites. Check with your technology coordinator to find out what works best for your school district.

Siegle (2002a) offered helpful tips for teachers incorporating e-portfolios in their classroom:

- Involve students in the process and practice division of labor.
- Start students at an early age.
- Spread selection [of pieces] over time.
- Back up the disks.
- Download digital images to the disk.
- Keep visual files small. (p. 62)

How can I use e-portfolios in my classroom?

1. Have students create an ongoing digital dialogue of their accomplishments over the course of the school year. Students may want to pick one or two of their best pieces each month to add to their e-portfolio as testament to their work.

2. Ask students to evaluate their strengths (and weaknesses) based on their e-portfolios. This helps them focus on what they are doing well, in addition to noting where improvement can be made throughout the year.

3. Begin helping students plan for future careers by having students highlight work that may relate to their field of interest.

4. Use e-portfolios as a multimedia tool for students to express their accomplishments. Allow students to use digital cameras to take pictures of their three-dimensional work, scan and upload copies of other items, and use software such as iMovie, PowerPoint, Photoshop, and Illustrator to enhance the work featured in their e-portfolios.

> 5. Share e-portfolios with parents at the end of the year to display students' learning and achievement. Allow students to present their e-portfolio to their parents and classmates and explain why they chose the pieces included in their portfolio.

Wikis

Working together toward a common goal is one of the skills students learn as they get acquainted with Web tools. A *wiki* (from wiki-wiki, meaning "quick" in Hawaiian) is one of these tools. A wiki gives users the freedom to create and edit Web page content using any Web browser (Wetzel, 2008). It allows students to enter the world of instant publishing where they can edit, delete, and add online content. Wikis are tools that can be used to collaborate on projects from a distance. In the classroom, it makes it easier to begin a project, see its progression, and complete it in less time.

Wikis are collections of Web pages that are linked together, and they can be edited by anyone who has access to them. Collaborators can add new content, edit existing content, add links to know Web sites on the Internet, and create and link to new pages within the wiki. They also can add graphics, video and audio files, calendars, and chat features. The wiki is a shared repository of knowledge. (Siegle, 2008, p. 14)

Wiki projects can introduce students to a whole new world where students live and think differently than they do in their hometown. Cultural diversity opens up new perspectives on ideas and can be motivating. Wikis also give everyone a voice in an assignment, even if it is the simple act of deleting or adding a sentence to the page. Wikis are based on collaboration, and students can learn the skill at an early age.

The audience drives the wiki. In most cases, users share a common interest or goal. Users form communities where conversations and ideas are exchanged as topics grow toward consensus. Businesses use wikis for developing projects; for example, online auction giant eBay has added a wiki function to its e-commerce site. Teachers can use wikis for professional development and other issues regarding education.

In the school setting, it can present an opportunity to bring students together for collaboration. It can be used in a classroom, or even used to plan a project with two different classrooms where each class or student has input. Dividing classes into teams can offer more opportunities for different points of view. That connection can lead to other projects with additional classrooms, neighboring schools, and students in other states and around the world. Wikis in Education (http://wikisineducation. wetpaint.com) helps connect teachers with others who are interested in collaborating on projects.

There are many positives to using wikis with students. Wikis provide kids with a platform to express their ideas in a project-based activity. The open-endedness of the wiki often makes it easier to express ideas and embellish others. Wikis permit students to begin a project and see it completed in a shorter amount of time due to the collaboration component. In addition, although not all students have trouble with organizational skills, some do. Wikis can help them organize their thoughts as they work with their peers on different projects. Wikis also allow kids to express their feelings on an issue while learning to accept the opinions of others in written form as they work together.

The wiki can be used in the classroom in a variety of ways. A group of students from Magnolia, TX, teamed its efforts with a class from Ohio to write a book online. The two classes took turns writing the chapters—one student simply picked up where another left off. The Wiki was a good choice for this project because it was easy for students to write and edit the book online.

Students in Nancy Bosch's sixth-grade gifted class in Shawnee Mission, KS, had finished reading *The Wright 3* by Blue Balliett. Because the teacher only saw these students one full day a week, time was at a premium. She wanted her students to write a reflection essay on what they had learned by reading the book, in addition to gathering more information about aspects of the book that interested the students, and decided to use Wikispaces (http://www.wikispaces.com), a free site that is ad-free. (Another free site for educators without ads is PBwiki at http://pbwiki.com/edu.wiki.) Within one day, all 17 students were set up on Wikispaces and were ready to work on their essays. She introduced them to Wikipedia and other resources, where they practiced conducting effective searches on the Internet. The students were excited about the project, and it opened an opportunity to discuss copyright issues, note-taking techniques, and plagiarism.

For this project, Bosch had students work in pairs, and each student pair had its own page to work on. Students had to add or delete items and save their work. Over a period of five hours, all seventeen students finished their work on *The Wright 3*. They enjoyed writing their wikis and produced a lot of information for others to read about the book (see http://thewright3.wikispaces.com).

Wetzel (2008) suggested using Wikis in science class opens up all kinds of learning possibilities. Among these is the creation of a glossary. Students can add new terms to the glossary throughout the school year. Students can report their findings to the teacher while learning how to collect data and negotiate findings with other classmates or collaborate with other schools to collect data on science projects. Wikis give science students the chance to take ownership in their own learning and become more actively engaged in the scientific process.

Wikis are a good option for students who enjoy using computers and collaborating with others. A collaborative writing project similar to the one in which students from Ohio and Texas participated can be one way to integrate this tool in the classroom. It is important to note, however, that some students may not work well in a collaborative environment (Siegle, 2008). Many students prefer working alone, or may be embarrassed to have their work out in the open for others to critique and edit. Be flexible when assigning collaborative projects and be sensitive to students' learning styles and needs. Students who have had a chance to get to know one another and attain a certain level of trust make this type of project easier (Howard, 2000).

How can I use wikis in my classroom?

1. Create an "About me" wiki that students contribute to at the beginning of the school year so students (and teachers) can get to know the class (Siegle, 2008).

2. Ask students to use wikis to collaborate on writing projects with other students, whether in their school or with a partner school from a different state or country.

3. Have students develop a wiki that shares information about specific content they have learned in class, reflecting what they have learned during their study.

4. Have students work on individual wikis throughout the year that focus on their area of interest or passion. Allow them to share these with other students.

5. Allow science students to develop wikis to share data from their research and their findings from an experiment.

Social Bookmarking

"*Social bookmarking* is the practice of saving bookmarks to a public Web site and 'tagging' them with keywords [italics added]" (EDUCAUSE Learning Initiative, n.d., para. 5). Keywords pertaining to lessons, such as one on geometry, can be linked to Web sites that relate to that topic. Tagging items is just one aspect of social bookmarking. Teachers can tag topics they use in their curriculum, which can connect them with other teachers. Information also can be shared on current research in their field, making it easier to locate colleagues with like interests.

Social bookmarking is a tool that can help students do their research more effectively. It also gives them a chance to share their findings with their peers at the same time. Students can share bookmarks with one another and use them to gain insight into their topics of interest. It also can make the research process more interesting, as they are able to connect with peers who have the same interest they do.

Students (and teachers) must register with a social bookmarking site in order to use this tool. Some commonly used sites include:

- del.icio.us (http://delicious.com)
- Furl (http://www.furl.net)
- Ma.gnolia (http://ma.gnolia.com)
- Netvouz (http://www.netvouz.com)

It is best to research each site before making a decision as to which one works best for your classroom. Once students have registered with a social bookmarking Web site, they are then able to save bookmarks and retrieve them from any computer with access to the Internet.

How can I use social bookmarking in my classroom?

1. Have students bookmark sites related to their research projects. Buddy Marks (http://buddymarks.com; Jackson, 2006) is an online social bookmark manager. It's free and students can control who accesses their site by combining their tags with their own.

2. Engage students in peer-based learning where their interests drive the sites they are bookmarking. Create friendship-driven groups that use the concept of tagging to create community service projects like helping the homeless. Have the students initiate their own ideas of ways to be of service.

3. Have students do a career search on a future profession in which they are interested. Make the project ongoing, giving them a chance to see how their interests develop over time. They also will see how their tagged items will have changed over time.

4. Divide the class into teams to write a comparative essay on a topic based on their interests. Each student can conduct research and share their tagged bookmarks with other students in the group. Have them debate the differences found on their bookmarked sites.

5. Have students collaborate on a research project with other schools by sharing bookmarks among the participating schools or classes.

Educaching

Global Positioning Systems (GPS) and Geographic Information Systems (GIS) have been around since the 1960s. First used by the military, they are now part of the way we live our lives, from the cars we drive, to the games we play. This technology is now being used in nursing, space, and crime scene investigation professions, to name a few.

Geocaching is a game that is played worldwide where geo-cachers use GPS technology to locate "treasures" that have been placed for others to find using latitude and longitudinal coordi-nates and hints. These high-tech scavenger hunts use the Inter-net to help geocachers locate hidden caches (containers) that have been hidden in their community. Educaching refers to the educational use of geocaching.

For kids interested in "how things work," geocaching gives them the fun of the hunt. Teachers can align this challenging activity to the standards when they teach geography and science with GPS technology. Teachers can create scavenger hunts that solve riddles, math problems, and questions related to geography. These activities can be fun and motivating and increase deductive and inductive reasoning skills. Most importantly, kids enjoy such activities.

A cache is waterproof container that is used to hold objects and artifacts (Lary, 2004). Artifacts often are personal and say something about the person who left them. Some objects that have been found in caches are logbooks, toys, musical recordings, and photos.

Various caches can be found on Geocaching (http://www.geocaching.com), the official site for GPS caches. In order to locate nearby caches, enter your zip code, and a list of caches will appear. Each includes the latitude and longitude coordinates, as well as clues to its location. To participate in this "hunt" you will need some kind of a GPS (Global Positioning System). The GPS device receives signals from satellites that orbit the Earth, and cost anywhere from $100 to $1,000. The GPS acts as a compass and triangulates a location resulting in a global address. Devices in the $100-dollar range are the Garmin Yellow eTrex and the Magellan eXplorist. They are good choices for the classroom, and can be purchased through grant monies if there isn't a budget for such devices.

After determining which cache the students will locate, its coordinates are entered into the GPS system, the clues are read, and the hunt begins. However, before allowing students to begin the hunt, teachers must prepare them for using the GPS device. A lesson explaining how it works and practice entering latitude and longitude coordinates is vital before students can take part in geocaching.

Hubbard (2007) prepared his students by explaining the GPS concepts and making them aware of his expectations for the activity. He also explained the 3 R's of GPS etiquette: learning how to *respect* the area, taking *responsibility* for what students find, and being willing to *replace* what they have found. He also emphasized that a teacher can take any lesson and adapt it to this technology, as long as they have access to the equipment and are able to locate containers that are without cost.

Students will use the GPS system to locate the "treasure." Once they have found it, they should sign their names to the logbook and return everything to the container for the next person to locate it. Once they are back in the classroom, students will need to be debriefed and discuss any challenges they experienced. Geocaching is an extension of learning, and students can use their computers for extended research and create demonstrations based on their findings (Hubbard, 2007).

Shaunessy and Page (2006) offer advice for future hunts:

Following this initial experience with learning to use the GPS system, teachers can hide caches, develop clues, and distribute the clues to students prior to their quest. . . . Once students have had experience searching for teacher-created caches, they are ready to design their own caches by selecting an appropriate container, cache items, and possibly a theme for the cache. Student teams can collaborate by writing challenging clues to locate the caches.

This allows students to be engaged in the planning of the hunt and enjoy the rewards of a successful search. (p. 51)

The following sites contain helpful information about geocaching:

- All About GPS Tutorial (http://www.trimble.com/gps/index.html)
- Geocaching With Kids (http://www.eduscapes.com/geocaching/kids.htm)
- GIS and GPS Lesson Plan Resources (http://www.gis2gps.com/GIS/lessons/lessons.html)
- GPS Guide for Beginners http://www.garmin.com/aboutGPS/manual.html

How can I use geocaching in the classroom?

1. Develop your own caches in which parts of a story are placed in different areas, and students have to find all of caches to put the story together.

2. Have students develop their own caches and the clues to go along with them. Set up a hunt for younger students, and have your students teach the younger students the basic concepts involved in geocaching.

3. Use geocaching to teach students about maps, how to locate landmarks, and longitude and latitude.

4. Have students use Google Earth to locate their home using longitude and latitude.

5. Have students develop a geocaching tour of their town that takes people to different monuments, statues, or markers of historical events, and leave a narrative for each location in the cache (Utah Coalition for Educational Technology, 2008).

These technologies usually are part of the "need to know" list for tech-savvy students. It is not unusual for them to keep their teachers up-to-date on new technology that is coming out. They know about the product, anticipate its arrival, and may already know how to use it. These tools are more than just something they want; they are something they need to expand their growing understanding and use of technology tools that are available to them. Providing students with a variety of technology tools that are available will not only make their learning more individualized, it will create a classroom that is rich in an entrepreneurial spirit.

Combining Technology and Simulations

"Personally, I'm always ready to learn, although I do not always like being taught."

—Winston Churchill

THE middle school students from a small town in Georgia were immersed in a simulation activity. They were involved in a mock trial that had all of the makings of reality TV. The trial centered on the controversy associated with eminent domain. The town had experienced a number of legal battles associated with the destruction of private homes to revitalize the downtown area and the decision had directly affected a number of students and their families. With this in mind, the class was about to put the town on trial. Using a simulation as a teaching tool, the conflict presented an ideal way to experience real-world issues.

Students were introduced to courtroom procedure through the mock-trial simulation. They learned about the rules of evidence, basic facts, and statements given by witnesses. Students were selected to participate in the roles of the attorneys, judge, bailiff, court reporters, and jurors (Arbetman & O'Brien, 1978).

In an effort to give the students a look at what it takes to come to an agreement, the teacher tried something new. She had the class use a wiki as the tool that would decide fate of the accused. The wiki was chosen so jurors could contribute ideas to a growing document about the issues surrounding the trial. Jurors submitted their statements containing thoughts about the evidence in an effort to help reach a decision. This simulation was also extended using Skype (http://www.skype.com), a free communication software that lets you talk or make video calls online. Through Skype, students took a virtual field trip, interviewing a real-life judge to discuss the issue of eminent domain.

This type of classroom simulation integrates technology into the activity. Online simulations can teach students about frog anatomy through dissection, show what it is like to experience a virtual earthquake, and introduce math concepts that deal with inferences and predictions, among many other options.

Each day, the traditional classroom is faced with more and more students who spend their free time immersed in SimCity, SecondLife, Railroad Tycoon, or the most current gaming platform. These simulations offer students decision-making opportunities on a regular basis, and simulations also are beneficial in the classroom. Simulations, combined with teacher input and interaction from the students, can make a difference in the simulation's intent, student impact, and the way the activity is perceived. Students learn best when they are actively involved and when simulations achieve a real-world feeling.

Prensky (2007) referred to this concept as interactive pretending that allows learners to discover how systems behave in the world without touching them. The idea of doing new things in different ways is future oriented. Incorporating technology into the activities makes simulations a powerful choice for the classroom. Although simulations are not new to teachers and the classroom, technology has provided a way for students to experience these moments in real time through Web-based simulations, software-based simulations, or virtual simulations.

Web-based simulations allow students to experience events, many of them historical in nature. They learn how to problem solve as they gather data, collaborate on a problem, and develop a product. Many Web-based simulations allow students to get a glimpse of history by role-playing historical characters or governmental leaders.

Using software-based simulation games like SimCity, The Oregon Trail, and Civilizations, students are asked to make decisions in which the outcomes will be affected by the decisions they make.

Virtual field trips and interactive videoconferencing offer ways for your students to experience real-life situations. Scientific, medical, and corporate careers can now be shared with students who are interested in exploring these options. Making students part of this decision-making process can empower them and provide you with topics of current interest to engage students. With the help of your tech coordinator, these projects can be offered to other students with similar interests by "clustering" them from different geographic locations to experience the same field trip.

The Interactive Communications and Simulations Group at the University of Michigan (http://ics.soe.umich.edu) offers a number of Web-based programs for high school students that introduce them to simulation gaming, activism, service learning, and social networking. The projects connect students, mentors, and facilitators through character play, self-expression, and social activism. Simulations are offered in a number of different venues. For example, a simulation available on the Arab-Israeli conflict immerses students in national and international politics. The simulation currently is made up of 16 three-character teams, which comprise high-level government or political figures. The simulation introduces students to real-world diplomacy, is reality based, and gives students a stronger insight into the gravity of an international conflict.

The possibilities for simulations are endless and permit a teacher to develop a scenario around a current event that he or she can use in the classroom. For instance, Rimes (2007) created a framework for a lesson on copyright infringement after Steve Vander Ark was sued for trying to publish a book called *Harry Potter Lexicon*.

"*Harry Potter* Lawsuit—You Be the Judge!" provided teachers with a way to present a lesson on copyright vs. fair use issues. Students researched articles, media, and images related to copyright issues and this particular case in an effort to determine their own position on the topic. Using a multimedia tool, like PowerPoint, students were asked to pull together a visual essay as to whether they agreed with the actual real-life decision.

This type of lesson can be taken a step further by including other technology such as wikis to arrive at consensus or set up a blog so students can share their perspectives on issues such as the *Harry Potter* copyright case.

Virtual worlds have opened up a new perspective on simulations that are engaging, collaborative, and cutting edge. Second Life and its sister site Teen Second Life are Internet-based virtual environments. These online virtual worlds are three-dimensional and made up of residents called avatars, virtual characters created by each member. In these virtual worlds, adults and teens, respectively, can meet peers from all over the world, with a desire to create a world better than the one they know. They work together to build virtual structures on virtual real estate. Teen Second Life is only available for students ages 13–17, with built-in safeguards to protect students and there is a cost (although a basic account is free). In addition to the cost factor, schools with older computers may not have the video processing capabilities to run Second Life (Trotter, 2008).

Virtual worlds let students experience role-playing while collaborating and working with others. Students become part of the environments and are not just passive observers. These simulations are being used in distance education and self-paced tutorials, providing a platform for collaborative projects and discussions at the university level.

Simulations are a powerful tool that gets students involved in real-world situations. They allow students to gain insight into problems and aid in their decision-making process. Simulations imitate life. Working with one another to find a solution gives the process a sense of realism. Simulations also deal with mathematical and science concepts. The Princeton Plasma Physics Laboratory (http://www.pppl.gov) provides simulations for students with an interest in nuclear fusion. Before they can conduct virtual experiments, however, they need to have some kind of background in the subject. It is a safe way to explore the properties of nuclear fusion, and acts as a tutorial for students who need additional help.

Simulations work well for all students. Critical thinking strategies expand what they already know and they are able to look at the topic from more than one perspective.

Keys to Running a Simulation

The following information should be kept in mind while preparing simulations for the classroom.

1. Be sure there are enough roles for each student, even if they participate as audience members or observers.

2. Once the simulation has played out, be sure to call the students together to discuss what has taken place. Because some simulations can be highly emotional, facilitating a discussion is necessary. A lot of different perceptions may be occurring and need to be clarified.
3. Teachers should be flexible during the simulation and answer questions as they happen, if possible. This will help young children determine fantasy from reality.
4. Take time to ask questions at the end of the session. Students also need to provide input and explain their impression of what took place. Keep in mind that students likely will have more than one viewpoint.
5. Use open-ended questions to encourage discussion. If an event is filled with emotion and conflict, there may be a tendency to point fingers. Refrain the tendency to arrive at one conclusion.
6. Have students act out their part on what they know. Encourage them to back up their role based on research. This may not be as easy with elementary students, but they should be able to tell you about the character.
7. Parents and assistants may be used to help elementary students. Be sure to communicate with everyone ahead of time so they understand where they are needed (United States Institute of Peace, 2008).

Once you understand the basic idea of conducting a simulation in your classroom, then the creativity comes in. Simulations can incorporate all kinds of technology (see Chapter 3 for information on current technology in the classroom), thus making these real-world experiences even more meaningful to the tech-savvy learner.

Telementoring, Virtual Teams, and Distance Learning

"Smooth seas do not make skillful sailors."

—African Proverb

LIAM had been sitting at the computer for hours, visiting one Web site after another. He was consumed with extreme climate change and predictability, and believed the melting of the West Antarctic ice sheet could be maintained. At least, this is what he found according to the research he had conducted as a high school student.

He needed to find a university that would prepare him to be part of climatology research teams, and he also wanted to do an independent study with a professor working with climate change. It could be the motivation he needed to get him through the year. Liam lived in a small town in Nebraska, and trips to the state university just were not practical. Even with the Internet at his disposal, he needed more. Using his negotiating skills, he convinced his science teacher to help create a better option for him by allowing him to do an independent study. As luck would have it, his science teacher had connections with a university that offered a degree in Earth sciences and environmental engineering. Together they were able to set up a telementoring program with a professor that introduced him to future career options. As a result, his interest in climate change increased and upon graduation, he entered Columbia University in New York.

For many of today's students, the Internet is more than just a way to connect with peers. It is a venue for sharing projects, expressing viewpoints, and networking (McNulty, 2005). These students are content creators: They display their own artwork and photography, share their opinions with friends through blogging and social networking sites, and understand multimedia and how to use it (Lenhart & Madden, 2007). Web publishing has changed the way students write and made their writing purposeful (D. Hogue, personal communication, April 2006). Today's classroom is introducing students to the corporate world through telementor programs; to the world of business through the introduction of tech teams; and providing international connections through distance learning.

Telementor programs, virtual teams, and distance learning are providing an option for students with an in-depth interest or career focus that cannot be met in their hometown, state, or even country. Global learning is no longer just a concept. Issues connecting society and those trying to solve society's problems are a click away from emerging research and organizations.

Telementoring

For Marcia Clark, a high school student from the small town of Hoyt, KS, telementoring was the beginning of a big dream and a future goal. She wanted to create a frozen food delivery service for adults ages 65 and above who faced health challenges. The Family, Career and Community Leaders Association of America (FCCLA; see http://www.fcclainc.org) State Competition provides an opportunity for students to learn how to take action in their community. As part of the competition, Marcia created her business plan with a 60-page portfolio and a 20-minute presentation. Passion and confidence were apparent as she made her presentation and her persistence paid off. She took the silver award for her school (Rivero, 2005).

Marcia was part of the International Telementor Program (ITP; http://www.telementor.org), which connects students with adult professionals to assist them with a project or career interest. The program creates agreements with corporations and organizations to provide students with online mentors. In Marcia's case, it was Michael Short, a Hewlett-Packard employee from Vancouver, Canada. He helped her with her paper, not only technically, but also by contributing additional pictures, Web sites, and facts that were essential to her project, which was all done online, using a secure Web site. In addition, he set up an opportunity for her to present her idea at a small development firm at Washburn University (Rivero, 2005). Short recognized Marcia's entrepreneurial spirit, and encouraged her throughout the project.

The idea of mentoring has been around for some time. Creation of the Internet has taken it one step further, providing a way to connect professionals and support students in a more productive manner, and technology has made it possible for students and mentors to come together from different geographical locations in a safe learning environment. Telementoring takes mentoring to a completely new level, connecting students with a virtual mentor. The virtual mentor assists them through a project or a career interest. It involves coordination on the part of the teacher and the district in an effort to secure safe telementorships. Like anything else on the Web, steps need to be taken to make sure students taking part in this activity are connected with mentors who have been checked out and approved to work with a student. The student and the telementor use e-mail, text, and video conferencing to work together, most often never meeting face-to-face.

More than 40,000 students from nine different countries have worked with online mentors since 1995, making the International Telementor Program a successful choice for students across the U.S. and around the world. Its project-based matches are a good fit for gifted students who are interest-driven and career-focused. Even though they may collaborate daily, students and mentors may live hundreds of miles apart. For teachers who want help in matching students and interests, it is a viable resource (Siegle, 2003).

Telementoring gives students a snapshot of real-world situations beyond their own community. It connects them with professionals who share the same interests and understand the importance of learning about topics from other perspectives. For gifted students who are focused on future careers, it can be a chance to discover how deeply they want to learn about a topic by designing a project based on their interests. It means connecting them with broadcasters, physicians, scientists, and professors—any type of working professional—willing to guide and develop a student's interest in a particular subject.

ITP redefines the way students learn and provides resources to help them as they identify and pursue their personal interests (Chen, 2002). Students involved in ITP's program are introduced to the way the corporate world does business. They form business relationships and learn how young professionals ask for help on the job. They also learn technical writing skills and soon begin to emulate the writing styles of those in the profession they are modeling, using appropriate industry vernacular and jargon.

ITP takes student interests to adult-world levels through connections that reach beyond the students' communities. They learn how to explore career aspirations and develop a professional network. Mentors use career plans to help participants outline career paths and verify their activities through letters of confirmation. Connecting students with corporate sponsors has made telementoring a powerful tool. The impact goes beyond one-day job shadowing experiences, as involved professionals commit to long-term projects that can extend from several weeks to a year.

As mentioned previously, cybersafety issues are very important in telementoring programs. ITP is not a social mentoring program, and no personal information is shared. All mentors are employees of sponsor organizations, such as Merck, The George Lucas Foundation, and Pitney Bowes, and all correspondence is logged and monitored. This makes mentor-student communications easily accessible to parents, ITP staff, and teachers.

For gifted students, telementoring is another way to help them become more self-directed learners. Students work with mentors to articulate an interest and create a plan for their research. They get the opportunity to interview experts and develop a product related to their research interests. In many cases, they present their findings to an authentic audience.

Designing Your Own Telementoring Program

There are many aspects to think about when developing a telementoring program for your students. Most likely, not all of your students will participate in the program. This should be reserved for those students who have a passion for a particular topic and have the ability and stamina to work on it in depth for an extended period of time. Keep in mind:

- Students with an interest or passion for a particular subject may already have a topic they want to pursue. Encourage students to negotiate their ideas and to research organizations and corporations that pertain to their interests.
- Create a Web-based connection. The connection can be career focused or content focused, linking career professionals with students.
- Cybersafety issues should include confidentiality for both parties. Have students write messages in Word, and reroute the mail through your own e-mail account to ensure safety and place the teacher in control (Callahan & Kyburg, 2005; this is especially important for younger students).
- Have the student create a timeline for the project, and ensure that they are developing realistic deadlines.
- Telementoring can be curriculum based and used in an independent study. Multiple mentors also can be used, although you will need to ensure that the mentors understand this arrangement should you choose to go this route. Some mentors may prefer to work with a student one-on-one, with no other mentor input.

Tips for teachers:

- Make sure the telementors understand the importance of confidentiality. You might require a waiver to be signed to ensure that confidentiality is kept.
- Create a Web site or handout that addresses important issues surrounding telementors' responsibilities. This provides your expectations for them as mentors up front. Inform telementors of their responsibilities and time commitment.

- Telementors should not share personal information with the student. E-mail correspondence, home address, and telephone numbers are considered off limits.
- Although some telementors may be local, others may be in neighboring towns, states, or countries. For the students' safety, under no circumstances should individual, face-to-face meetings be tolerated.
- Think about the telementor's purpose: Will the telementor be used to facilitate career issues or course content? Is the connection serving more as an independent study?
- You may want to request a background check, paid for by the telementor.
- Evaluate the student/telementor relationship midway through the project. Is everything working out as planned? Is the telementor a good fit with this particular student? Are both parties happy with the relationship?

Tips for telementors:
- Telementors are the link between a student's interest and passion for a topic. They can expand a student's knowledge of a subject and provide inspiration for self-directed investigations, so it is important for telementors to keep their commitments.
- E-mails should be short and informative. They can be open-ended for follow-up questions. Instant messaging also is an option. If students are involved in product development, they can use their cell phone to keep the telementor informed of their progress. Contact should be kept to a limited amount each week (e.g., 1–2 e-mails), as it can quickly become a huge time commitment for both the mentor and student should a limit not be set from the start.

- Telementors should ask questions that promote decision-making. For example, how do you feel about global warming? What are some strategies to create awareness? In addition, use questions that determine a student's understanding of his or her project. Is he able to convey what he is trying to do? Can he express his goals and explain how he is going to reach them? Help them articulate their ideas.

Teachers, as coordinators of a telementoring program, should maintain an ongoing relationship with all telementors and ensure that both mentors and students are happy with the program.

Virtual Teams

Teachers looking to create options for gifted students with computer talent may want to consider the teaming approach. Learning how to collaborate in virtual situations is a best practices tool used by businesses on a global scale (Carlino, 2005). "A virtual team is a group of people who work interdependently across space, time, cultures, and organizational boundaries on temporary, non-occurring projects with a shared purpose while using technology" (Smith, n.d., para. 2). Virtual teams form collaborative environments that cross time, boundaries, and countries. In fact, while working together to complete a project, most team members never meet (Lipnack, 2001).

Collaboration is nothing new for gifted students who are already connected by technology. These students always seem to find each other, and communicating across time and distance is second nature for them. Seventeen-year-old Devon, an entrepreneur from Virginia, learned the importance of collaboration to develop his business. The Internet opened up new worlds with contacts around the world, including an economist who studied virtual games and a businessman with insight on marketing strategies in Australia.

This teaming strategy can be used to cluster students with like interests while simulating the real world of business. Virtual teams use e-mail, chat, instant messaging, and teleconferencing to communicate. They may come from different geographic locations, but they have one goal in mind: to complete their project. They solve work-related issues and, at the same time, they learn how to work effectively with people remotely.

According to Eric Calvert, assistant director of instructional services and supports at the Ohio Department of Education, opportunities such as virtual teams can been effective tools in the classroom. They allow schools to form consortia to aggregate students with a very specific set of needs and interests, making it possible to provide a more individualized education while keeping a lid on costs. According to Calvert,

> Not only can it help connect students with experts and peers with similar interests, but it allows students to learn to use tools and media for which they already have an affinity. People persist with difficult, even frustrating, tasks when they're intrinsically motivated and are working in an area where their sense of self-efficacy is high. Therefore, when educators can let students use tools for learning that they enjoy and feel confident with, they can challenge students to engage more advanced curriculum and learn more independently than would otherwise be possible. (E. Calvert, personal communication, September 2008)

Creating Virtual Teams

Virtual teams are another way to introduce students to the world of collaboration. Real-world issues, at home or on a broader scale, are a way for students to see the larger picture. Teams can be clustered by having students from different classes in one school work together or can be dispersed at different school locations. The following information should be kept in mind when establishing virtual teams in the classroom:

- Select teams of no more than four to six students, as larger numbers can be difficult to manage. Students can be in middle school or high school.
- Create partnerships with technology teachers, gifted coordinators, gifted teachers, and content teachers, both locally and across the country (and even world) in order to team up students for a virtual team.
- Have students select a problem or an issue within their community that needs attention. The team will work together online to solve the issue. Students may want to market an item, increase awareness of an issue, or come up with their own idea. Students need to determine a desired outcome.
- Work with the students to create a realistic timeline.

Creating Team Charters

Charters were created as a way to help virtual teams solve problems. It is a plan that outlines the goals, individual strengths, expectations, and challenges that could determine the team's success or failure (Noble, 2008). A charter provides a number of choices for the team to solve problems. For example, if a team wanted to delve into issues that crossed cultural lines, they would have to address language barriers. Finding ways to offset those challenges will be outlined in the charter.

The charter looks at the team's individual strengths and provides a step-by-step plan with timelines to achieve their goal. It forces members to think ahead and see the problem as a whole, using different problem-solving strategies along the way. Ground rules also are identified, as well as options for dealing with conflicts within the team. It is a binding contract, and a good exercise in real-world business practices.

In short, virtual teaming provides tech-savvy students a window into the world of work using professional skill strategies.

Distance Learning

Expanding the boundaries of the traditional classroom has made a difference in the way students perceive issues, events, and day-to-day lessons. Distance learning is referred to by a number of terms, including *distance education*, *virtual learning*, *online learning*, and *video conferencing*. These tools bring the world to the classroom. "Distance learning transcends the constraints of time and space by using such media as computer- or Internet-based programs, which allow educators and learners to interact, but not necessarily in face-to-face situations" (Olszewski-Kubilius & Lee, 2004, p. 7). Distance learning allows schools to connect with each other, create virtual field trips, and share interactive seminars. Teachers also can take part in professional development.

There are various modes that connect students using distance learning, including e-mail, televised lectures, Web-based courses, streaming audios and videos, and electronic field trips (Olszewski-Kubilius & Lee, 2004). In addition, video conferencing allows people in different locations to connect "live" for programs, interviews, and events. Skype (http://www.skype.com), a communications software, is another option that can connect students. It allows students to make free calls over the Internet to other Skype users—with just a computer! This type of technology engages students by allowing them to network with others around the world. In some classrooms, distance learning is being used to practice foreign languages through teacher-mediated Web forums and collaborative projects. Technology has made Web-based distance learning convenient for anyone. Classes such as these can be completed anywhere, as long as there is an Internet connection available (Siegle, 2002b).

Online classes, digital charter schools, and virtual schools are removing barriers for gifted students that "don't fit" in the regular classroom. They also have created options for students where gifted services are not available and for students who would rather use their computers for something more than just connecting with their peers, doing some shopping, or downloading music.

Online learning began by offering courses to schools that wanted to increase choices for students to take coursework not offered by their home school. These courses take regularly scheduled classes and offer them in a way they can be taken and completed at a distance. Students participating in these classes continue to grow. According to Patrick (2008), in 2007, there were more than one million students enrolled in K–12 online learning programs in the United States, with growth rates increasing 30% annually. Student demand also is doubling, with enrollment for courses up more than 100%.

Many of these students are involved in virtual school programs. These schools can be associated with the Department of Education or serve as nonprofits and are fully accredited. Offerings can include middle school curriculum and high school courses, including Advanced Placement and college-prep level courses. There are a number of virtual charter schools that allow students to be taught from their home computer. These schools work well for young students, and those with schedules that need flexibility due to their involvement in sports and music. It also has been a plus for those that have experienced illnesses that have kept them out of school for lengthy periods of time.

Online learning creates possibilities for gifted students, allowing them to learn through technologies that permit them to exchange ideas, create new ones, and work on collaborative projects. Tech-savvy students enjoy connecting with one another and learning at their own pace. This environment challenges them and increases their global awareness, providing a venue for expression they understand.

These students are motivated by their ability to research information. Many like contributing to a larger group working on the same project. Changing, molding, and creating something new that can be used in other ways draws students to this kind of learning. In learning how to work together from a distance, students meet and communicate with others with like interests.

Virtual School Resources

There are currently a number on online programs that are available to gifted students.

Education Program for Gifted Youth Online High School (EPGY) at Stanford University. Stanford University's first online high school for gifted students is a 3-year program. It is fully accredited and grants diplomas. It is a positive educational option for gifted students across the U.S. and globally. Coursework is rigorous and is offered through the Internet. Classes focus on mathematics, natural sciences, and social sciences. Students can combine courses from their local schools with courses from the online high school. This is a tuition program. Full-time tuition (four or more classes) is $13,000, and part-time tuition (two or three classes) is $8,000 for the academic year. For more information, please visit http://epgy.stanford.edu/ohs.

Center for Talented Youth (CTY) at Johns Hopkins University. The Center for Talented Youth offers a distance education program, *CTYOnline*, which started in 1983. The program now serves more than 10,000 students. Courses include economics, mathematics, foreign language, and physical sciences. Courses are delivered through the Internet or CD-ROM. Each course is self-paced, permitting students to cover as much material as possible. The program also offers an international component, summer school options, and programs for younger students. Fees are charged for coursework and vary. For more information, please visit http://cty.jhu.edu/ctyonline.

Independent Study High School at the University of Nebraska–Lincoln. The University of Nebraska–Lincoln Independent Study High School offers rigorous college prep, core, elective, and Advanced Placement courses. Courses are designed for the average to high-ability level student reading at a grade-appropriate level. The program requires an adult to proctor exams, but certified teachers evaluate and grade the work. These online courses bridge the gap between high school and college. Fees are assessed for coursework taken. For more information, please visit http://nebraskahs.unl.edu.

Iowa Online Advanced Placement Academy (IOAPA). The Iowa Online Advanced Placement Academy offers Advanced Placement courses to students across the state. Courses are fully subsidized, but students must pay to take the AP exam. On-site school mentors work with students taking online courses and help students assess their progress. The program is in partnership with The Belin-Blank Center at the University of Iowa. Fees are assessed for coursework taken. For more information, please visit http://www.iowaapacademy.org.

University of Missouri Center for Distance and Independent Study Program. The high school program serves more than 8,000 students online. The courses include mathematics, science, language arts, and social studies. They also offer a number of Advanced Placement (AP) courses. All classes are student-centered, empowering students to take charge of their learning. Lessons are self-paced and include faculty- and computer-evaluated lessons. Gifted courses are designated by category due to increased rigor and expectations. Fees are assessed for coursework. For more information, please visit http://cdis.missouri.edu/programs.aspx.

The Virtual High School, Maynard, MA. The Virtual High School (VHS) provides net courses for high school students at the national and international level. Schools pay memberships to free up a teacher one period a day to teach a course for VHS Online. All teachers are certified in the courses they teach and classes are asynchronously weekly scheduled, permitting students to access their classes anytime of the day or night. Classes are offered for students in grades 9–12. Courses range from Maritime History to Constitutional Law, providing students with a wide range of topics. They also offer classes for middle school gifted and talented students. These classes run for 15 weeks with a strong emphasis on peer collaboration. For more information, please visit http://www.govhs.org/website.nsf.

Town Hall Lecture Series

Creating a distance learning program from the ground up is not an easy task, but that is exactly what Mary Ellen Amaral Carras did as the high school gifted coordinator for the Educational Service Center of Lorain County (ESCLC) in Elyria, OH.

For 75 years, Cleveland, OH, had offered a series of public lectures to educate and inform Ohio citizens with no political agenda. About 10 years ago, the Town Hall Lecture Series received funding to branch out and start a student matinee series, inviting local youth to attend lectures by nationally renowned speakers. Unfortunately, the student series' time slot was eventually changed to the evening, and student attendance waned. Overcommitted students and teachers with hectic schedules often found it a challenge to bring students downtown on a Monday evening to participate in the lecture series.

The Town Hall Lecture Series sought ways to increase its student attendance. Recognizing the need for a change, the Town Hall Board invited Carras to a breakfast to discuss ways to bolster student attendance. When brainstorming ideas to increase student attendance, Carras suggested adding an additional component to the series that would focus on interviews of the lecture series speakers during the school day and use interactive video distance learning to facilitate the process.

Because Carras had attended professional development distance learning sessions hosted by the ESCLC Tech Coordinators Dave Miller and Paul Hieronymus, she was familiar with the outreach that such technology affords. In addition, Town Hall had a partnership with WVIZ Studio in Cleveland, which agreed to broadcast the distance learning programs to classes throughout Ohio as well as welcome a live studio audience.

Carras suggested asking the guest lecturers if they would be willing to donate an hour of their time on the same days as their evening lecture commitment so that interviews could be disseminated through interactive distance learning programs on a national level—but during the school day. It also was an effective way for students to take part in the Town Hall question-and-answer sessions, as cost was not an issue. Distance learning video equipment was already factored into each school's connection costs, so no additional cost was incurred by participating high schools.

Soon, the answer became clear: Make the students part of the actual programming. If gifted students from multiple schools across the region could form a collaborative leadership team, then they could plan, write, host, and publicize the programs themselves. Partnerships with guidance counselors, administrators, and teachers helped to identify students with interests in politics, world events, and technology who may be interested in participating in this series, and the first Town Hall Youth Council (THYC) was formed in 2003, with Carras and Mark Olson, Town Hall board member, as coadvisors.

Soon, there was active involvement with the speakers. Dr. Robert Arnot, a former NBC news medical correspondent who had just returned from the front, agreed to be an initial speaker. The students also interviewed Dr. William Schultz, Executive Director of Amnesty International. His topic, "How Civil Rights Affects Us All," was broadcast to 35 schools and 700 students across Ohio. Other speakers included political speech writer and TV/movie celebrity, Ben Stein; former Consul General to Saudi Arabia, Gina Abercrombie-Winstanley; first female President of Ireland, Mary C. Robinson; The Capitol Steps satirical comedy team; and many other journalists, scientists, and world leaders.

The students were actively involved in an authentic learning project. They had to assume responsibility of creating a program from the ground level: They wrote the scripts for the programs, researched the featured speaker's biography, delivered it using distance learning equipment, originated questions to launch the student discussion, facilitated the question-and-answer session that followed, and closed each show. Other students wrote articles for the press and operated the incoming questions from student viewers who e-mailed them to the station during the speaker's presentation (M. Carras, personal communication, November 2006).

Prior to taking part in the Town Hall Lecture Series, approximately 90% of the students had not been involved with distance learning. Interactive video sessions opened up an entirely new world to students—one they never knew existed. Learning how to use the equipment to conduct long-distance planning meetings and be part of the programming gave the sessions real-world implications. Moreover, the seminars were more than just a lesson in other key ways: Managing the technology and communication provided students with important leadership skills.

Students on the council wanted to have an even greater impact on their peers by starting a student-run seminar for gifted high school students in their county. As a result, Carras decided to rent space at Lorain County Community College (LCCC) and host a 250-student seminar each year. Limited funding was needed, and Carras was awarded a grant from the Educational Service Center Endowment Fund to finance costs. Topics varied from "Homelessness in Our Area" to "Health Issues That Confront Teens." For their first seminar, students hosted Ohio Senator Sherrod Brown and utilized distance learning to satellite the session to several schools that could not attend. In

2007, the council used interactive video distance learning to connect with 20 high school students from Israel to discuss the impact of war on their respective nations. The following year, the council used distance learning to enhance the seminar "Issues in Africa: A Closer Look," which connected student attendees with Lost Boys from the Sudan as well as the Brown University Kenya Medical Exchange Program in Providence, RI. Finally, 2009's council provided an interior look into a live robotic surgery from The Cleveland Clinic, featuring its robot, the DaVinci, which performed a renal surgery for all 250 students to witness from their seats in LCCC. To end this seminar, titled "New Frontiers: Alternatives in Energy, Health Care, and the Environment," the council hosted ocean environmentalist, Philippe Cousteau, whom they had interviewed earlier that year at WVIZ. Philippe spoke to the students from Florida about issues confronting the ocean environment and engaged students in a question-and-answer session as well.

The experience gained through exposure to world-renowned leaders surpassed any classroom lecture on the same topic. Students incorporated these authentic learning experiences into college admission and scholarship essays and were awarded many opportunities for acceptance into select colleges as well as scholarship funding accompanying the admissions offers. According to Carras, "THYC was a venue for cognitively gifted students to meet other students of similar interests who also needed a shot in the arm or an escape from the norm of four classroom walls to reignite their academic fire" (M. Carras, personal communication, November 2006).

Although not every classroom or school may be able to develop an interactive distance learning program such as this one, it is something to consider. When planning something like this, even on a smaller scale, here are some important things to keep in mind:

- Collaborate with your district's distance learning coordinator and a local television studio should you want the programs broadcast over an extended distance or throughout multiple communities.
- Create an advisory committee that will best outline the goals of your community for a program such as this.
- Have guidance counselors, administrators, and teachers provide names of students that could fit the profile of a student leader, as well as those students who may have interest in working with technology on this level.
- Have students write and facilitate the program. Students will need guidance from a teacher or other adult as they prepare to tackle the multifaceted issues that are involved in developing a distance learning program like the Town Hall Lecture Series.
- Fund the program through various local and/or federal grants should additional funding and resources be needed.

The Town Hall Lecture Series empowered students through leadership, communication, and team building. These forums forced students to "think on their feet" and adapt to the situation. Real-world topics and names in the news make distance learning a tool worth investigating. Issues pertaining to other cultures and countries, the environment, and authors are only a few of the options available for students ready and waiting to confront the issues in the world in which they live.

Advocating for the Tech-Savvy Student

"I skate to where the puck is going to be, not to where it has been."

—Wayne Gretsky

HER teacher often stared in amazement. The teacher had even invited the technology coordinator to come over and observe this student. Watching Gina was not only a pleasure, it was necessary: She understood the computer in a way most students envied. Teachers had been keeping an eye on her for years, but now it was even more critical. She was picking up on things beyond the staff's capabilities and was becoming quite bored in class. Often learning on her own, she had a deep passion for technology and liked the way she could get lost just researching topics.

A solution was reached: Signing up for online classes was a good choice for Gina, as they were able to meet her needs, and change her perception about school and learning. It was not always this way. Gina's relationship with the school system had been turbulent and depressing. She had no friends, and her teachers had pretty much written her off until they created a plan for her that addressed both her strengths and weaknesses.

When given an option, students with technology talent are empowered by decisions that emphasize their strengths. So, who are these kids? We are still learning about them, but technology teachers, gifted teachers, and the regular classroom teacher agree they have some traits in common. In order to advocate for them, you need to know who they are. Maybe they are already part of your classroom. Here are some characteristics of tech-savvy students:

- They are technologically fluent. They are at ease with the computer and know how to navigate it in order to get what they need. They are equally at ease with other new tools that come on the market.
- They have an understanding of how the computer works. These students often are the classroom technicians.
- Many of these students find their technology tools more compatible than being with their peers.
- They have a great passion about what they know and an understanding of technology, and willingly share their information with others.
- Some of these students also have strengths in math and music.
- They demonstrate entrepreneurship.
- They can find creative ways to use the computer if given the time—sometimes not to their advantage.
- They take a leadership role in projects that deal with technology.
- They just do not understand why some people "don't get it."

As a teacher, advocating for these students creates an awareness of the skills students have already mastered and their growing ability to handle assignments with increasing levels of difficulty. Connecting with colleagues and the technology coordinator can be a positive way to promote a student like Gina and her strengths in the school, and increase a general understanding of gifted students with the rest of the staff. In some cases, students with similar strengths will come up in the conversation and an opportunity presents itself to discuss their needs as well.

Students who are talented in technology and know about online learning may have already investigated the possibilities. Do not be surprised if they bring up the subject. Online learning merges the fields of gifted and talented education and information technology (Mulrine, 2007). Tech-savvy learners who are gifted demonstrate characteristics that are compatible with what we know about gifted students (Austega, n.d.).

Tech-Savvy Learners	Gifted Characteristics
1. Entrepreneurial	1. Entrepreneurial
2. Problem solvers	2. Sense when a problem exits
3. Interest driven	3. Strong focus on areas of interest
4. Technologically fluent	4. Learn rapidly and easily
5. Resourceful	5. Take leadership positions
6. Provide technical support	6. Are resourceful
7. Use computers in creative ways	7. Creative
8. Share what they know willingly	8. Retain and uses information they have
9. Are product savvy	9. Ask for assistance

Tech-savvy learners also are motivated by machines. They are fascinated by the way things work and can troubleshoot problems that relate to software and hardware. They are able to help those who are more technically challenged. Teaching peers forces them to question their own understanding of the subject by explaining the concept to another student, teaching them tolerance and understanding.

Being an advocate for gifted students who are technologically fluent can make a difference in the plans they have for the future. Use the suggestions below as a springboard to promote student abilities, and ask them for additional ideas. They are sure to have some!

- Understand the student's capabilities when it comes to technology.
- Use the technology standards as a way to assess their skill levels.
- Be willing to discuss their use of applications with other teachers.
- Share ways they integrate technology into their assignments with other teachers they may have.
- Discover ways to supplement interests, using enrichment, virtual mentorships, or competitions.
- Collaborate with school personnel to promote student abilities and increase awareness of students with needs outside the regular classroom.
- Become a resource for staff members with questions about advanced computer abilities.

Sternberg (1990) argued that giftedness is made up of multiple components, but there are also multiple forms of giftedness. Technology is changing the way we see giftedness. It has also changed the way we teach. The strategies we exercise in the classroom can be a powerful tool. Chances are, that tech-savvy student can help if you need it.

PART II

Facilitating High-Interest Learning

"Excellence is not an act, but a good social habit developed by a positive approach to maximum potential learning. Gifted education is not an honor or a privilege, it is a need."

—J. Clark

THEY were at it again. Three students were clustered around the computer in Mr. Linn's class and, as usual, were drawing a crowd. They were trying to find solutions for problems that were part of the New Jersey Institute of Technology's (NJIT) High School Programming Contest (http://cs.njit.edu/news/programmingcontest). This group had been together a long time. They learned about games at an early age and it just seemed natural to see what they could do together when given the chance. Truth was, this group had already made a reputation for themselves as tech-savvy students.

Ethan seemed to be "on-call" with most of his peers. In fact, there wasn't much he didn't know about the computer. He could fix just about anything and this placed him in a popular position. At times, even the staff members sought his help. Marissa saw patterns in numbers. She loved math and technology and made sense out of sequences that even amazed her teachers. Ryan was the "gamer" of the group. His adventuresome spirit kept him on the edge of making ethical decisions when it came to his abilities. He already could see his future: working for Google.

All three had an understanding of C++ and Java, so collaborating to compete in the NJIT High School Programming Contest was a natural choice.

Students like Ryan, Marissa, and Ethan have needs that involve more than one teacher. Their school's block schedule, consisting of 81 minutes, gave them more time in their classes and Mr. Linn provided enrichment opportunities to cut down on boredom. The high school also had additional measures in place that provided alternative options. Their school had created partnerships with nearby universities where they could enroll for additional coursework. They also could partner with a university mentor. Students were placed in internships, many of which were virtual. They were introduced to conflict resolution and taught how to handle political situations. They also learned the concept of philanthropy and the importance of "giving back." More than just a graded school system, these students were actively engaged in the world of adulthood, learning early on how to be contributors in their field.

Technology integration has taken the learning process to another level. For gifted students, technology applications have taken research beyond the computer, allowing teachers to incorporate authentic experiences into their teaching, and, in some cases, enable students to follow their interests through their own initiative.

The teachers featured in this section have selected a lesson that showcases technology in one of the subjects they teach. Each lesson is linked to state standards, giving any teacher an opportunity to connect it to his or her specific need.

Contents

Animal Writings by Debra Parkes—Grades 1–3 language arts...... 96

Endangered Species by Cindy Sheets—Grades 1–4 science....... 102

Jamestown: A Historical Role Play
by Kenneth J. Smith, Ph.D.—Grades 1–4 social studies 116

False Faces by Angela Ardoin—Grade 5 social studies........... 123

States Within the U.S.: Making Connections
by Sandra Cookson—Grade 6 geography/history............ 130

Shapes Are All Around Us
by Sharon Leamy—Grades 6–8 math (geometry) and science... 135

Digital Vocabulary by Eppie Snider—
Grades 6–8 computer science 140

Making History by David McDivitt—
Grades 9–12 world history and sociology 145

Stop Motion Pro by Rob Stetson—Grades 9–12 computer science ..151

Images of Deceit by Craig Wargowsky—
Grades 9–12 social studies and art....................... 158

Creating the Utopian Society by Diane Witt—
Grades 10–12 language arts 166

Animal Writings

By Debra Parkes

Grade Level
Grades 1–3

Overview

During grades 1–3, students begin learning the basics of word processing. They learn how to change the fonts, colors, and sizes of text, as well as alignments. They also begin learning how to add graphics from a file or clip art. This project is a creative way for them to use the five steps of the writing process (prewriting, writing, editing, proofreading, and publishing), develop their word processing skills, and work on point of view within writing. The final draft of the animal writing will be a written work in the shape of an actual animal of their choice (see Figure 1). For example, students could choose a cat and write from that cat's point of view. However, this project is not limited to animals. Any picture will do and this can be integrated with almost any subject (e.g., a science project could be a picture of a volcano with students becoming the volcano, describing what a volcano is made of, what makes it erupt, and so forth). This project could be an extension for a research project or practice for writing a story with a beginning, middle, and end using one object's point of view.

Figure 1. Example of a successful animal writing.

Objectives

1. Students will use the five steps of the writing process.
2. Students will write in the point of view of the chosen object.
3. Students will create a story about their object using correct grammar, spelling, and punctuation.
4. Students will write a story with a beginning, middle, and end.
5. Students will learn how to use the function keys in Word more effectively in order to form the shape of their chosen item.
6. Students will add a graphic behind the text in order to type on top of it.
7. Students will add a border using drawing tools.

8. Students will type their story using a keyboard.
9. Students will highlight the text and change the colors to coincide with those in the graphic underneath.

Standards Met

English Language Arts

1. Students adjust their use of spoken, written, and visual language (e.g., conventions, style, vocabulary) to communicate effectively with a variety of audiences and for different purposes.
2. Students participate as knowledgeable, reflective, creative, and critical members of a variety of literacy communities.
3. Students use spoken, written, and visual language to accomplish their own purposes (e.g., for learning, enjoyment, persuasion, and the exchange of information).

Technology

1. Students use keyboards and other common input and output devices (including adaptive devices when necessary) efficiently and effectively.
2. Students determine when technology is useful and select the appropriate tool(s) and technology resources to address a variety of tasks and problems.
3. Students use general purpose productivity tools and peripherals to support personal productivity, remediate skill deficits, and facilitate learning throughout the curriculum.
4. Students use technology resources (e.g., calculators, data collection probes, videos, educational software) for prob-

lem solving, self-directed learning, and extended learning activities.

Materials

- A computer with a word processing program (Microsoft Word is suggested)
- Access to graphics, either from a file, clip art, or the Internet
- Color printer

Procedure

1. Depending on the focus of your lesson (animals or another topic), students should pick an object that will become the focus of their story. They can locate a picture of their object using the Internet, or pick one out from ones you've previously chosen and have on hand in a file or clip art.

2. Guide students through the five steps of the writing process (prewriting, writing, editing, proofreading, and publishing) as they write a story from their object's point of view. They are to write as if they are the animal in the picture, and it can either be a story about the animal or facts about it—the more creative, the better. This most likely will take a few class periods as they work their way through the process and write a story they can "publish."

3. After the students have finished writing their stories, have them open a word processing program such as Microsoft Word. Ask them to use the drawing tools to create a border filled with color and then a white box in the middle of the page. Both the

outside box and the inside white box need to be formatted to be behind text so that the clip art (or any other graphic) can be seen.

4. Have students insert their graphic, which needs to be formatted to be behind the text. After they have added their graphic, they need to resize it to about half the page. The white box may need to be changed to a different color depending on what colors will be used in the writing. For example, if a student has a picture of a penguin, the white writing won't show up on the white background, so he or she will need to change the white box to a different color that would contrast all of the other colors.

5. Once they have set up their picture, students are now ready to start typing on top of it. The writing should fit entirely on the picture itself (e.g., if there is a space between a dog's ears, then there needs to be spaces included in the text also). If the animal (or object) ends, they need to hit "enter" to move to the next line. This provides great practice in using a variety of function keys.

6. Once students are finished typing their story on the picture, they can then change the colors of the text to match those in the picture. They might choose to bold some letters in order to make a certain color stand out (e.g., for the eyes). If they decide to change fonts, they should do that before starting to type their animal story, as the text will reflow if they change it after they have finished typing (however, that does provide further word processing practice should they forget to change something while they are in the midst of typing).

Evaluation

The assessment for the final project should be broken down into a rubric covering at least five components: how the page was set up, whether the story was in the correct point of view throughout, whether correct grammar and punctuation was used, whether the story is in the shape of the chosen animal (i.e., students used the function keys effectively), and what the final product looks like (i.e., the colors match what was in the picture, etc.).

Summary

Creating these animal writings touches upon several different learning components. First of all, students learn a new, creative way to present information. They are given a chance to focus on writing in a different point of view and practice their word processing skills. There are many different ways to implement this lesson by using a variety of topics in addition to animals.

Endangered Species

By Cindy Sheets

Overview

This high-interest unit is designed to introduce young gifted students to technology applications that help in the learning process, as well as research and presentation skills. They will select an endangered animal, and use the Internet as one of their sources for research. A short report is written, and then is used to develop an essay or persuasive writing piece designed to encourage others to support efforts to save their endangered species. Finally, students create an advertising slogan using Microsoft's WordArt, a poster using Microsoft Excel, and a presentation to share with an audience. The presentation may be completed in Microsoft PowerPoint or other similar technology or may be presented without additional technology (e.g., song, skit, etc.). Interested students may want to extend their learning by participating in real-life efforts to save endangered wildlife at the completion of this project.

The lesson presented here will focus on the part of the unit where students create a slogan and poster using an Internet search engine, WordArt, and Excel. The research and written portion would be complete at this point in the unit.

Objective

1. Students will use Microsoft Excel to develop a poster with an advertising slogan to help save an endangered species.

Standards Met

English Language Arts

1. Students adjust their use of spoken, written, and visual language (e.g., conventions, style, vocabulary) to communicate effectively with a variety of audiences and for different purposes.
2. Students gather, evaluate, and synthesize data from a variety of sources (e.g., print and nonprint texts, artifacts, people) to communicate their discoveries in ways that suit their purpose and audience.
3. Students use spoken, written, and visual language to accomplish their own purposes (e.g., for learning, enjoyment, persuasion, and the exchange of information).

Science

1. Students should develop an understanding of the characteristics of organisms.
2. Students should develop an understanding of organisms and their environments

Technology

1. Students demonstrate a sound understanding of the nature and operation of technology systems.

2. Students use technology tools to enhance learning, increase productivity, and promote creativity.
3. Students use productivity tools to collaborate in constructing technology-enhanced models, prepare publications, and produce other creative works.

Materials

- Internet access
- Microsoft Excel
- Microsoft's WordArt
- Printer paper (photo paper if available)
- Poster board
- Other materials as needed

Procedure

Students will create a poster that includes an enlarged photo of their endangered animal and a slogan designed to persuade the audience.

1. Using a search engine such as Google, students should search for images of their endangered animal. Remind them to think about what key words to use in the search: "What are the most important words that should be included to get the results you want?" When they reach the search page (e.g., http://www.google.com), students should be reminded to click on "Images" in order to restrict their search to pictures.

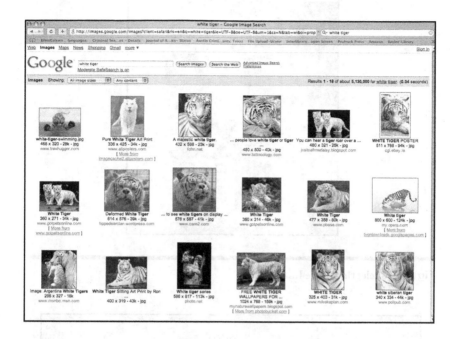

Figure 2. Sample results of an image search for "white tiger."

2. Students should search through the results to locate a high-quality image. In order to be clear when enlarged, look for images with the largest pixel size (see Figure 2).

3. When students have located an image to use, instruct them to right click with their mouse on the image, and select "Save Picture As." (On a Mac, students can hold down the Control key, click their mouse, and then select "Save Image As"; see Figure 3.) Make sure that the picture is being saved in the correct location or note where it is being saved (e.g., "My Pictures" or the student's folder). Students should give the picture a name that they will recognize later (e.g., "White Tiger"). Remind students that if they save more than one picture, unique names should be

Figure 3. Selecting "Save Image As."

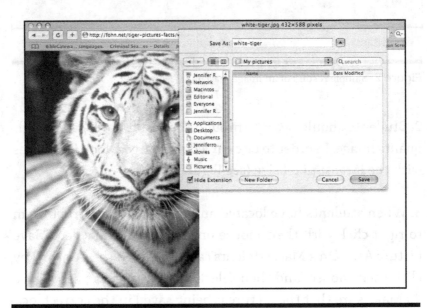

Figure 4. Saving a picture to a specific folder.

used (e.g., "White Tiger 1," "White Tiger 2," "White Tiger Cub").
See Figure 4.

4. After selecting a picture, students are now ready to begin designing their slogan. Have them think about the picture(s) they have located, and then think about their particular animal and how they might persuade someone to save it. Remind students that slogans are short and memorable. Ask students to brainstorm slogans they know (e.g., "Just Do It"; "Have It Your Way"; "I Can't Believe It's Not Butter!"). Share more samples of slogans using commercials found online or prerecorded from your TV. Discuss how rhyming, alliteration, and word play are important concepts in developing slogans. Talk about how these forms can be used to enhance a slogan. Have students brainstorm slogans for their endangered species. They should come up with several ideas, and see which works best.

5. Students should create their poster using Microsoft Excel, following these steps (if students are more advanced and would prefer to use different software to make their posters, allow them to do so):
- Open a new Excel document.
- Click on the "View" menu on the top tool bar and select "Normal."
- Now click on "View," then "Zoom," and go to 25% (or click on the percent tool if it is showing in the toolbar and go to 25%).
- What you should see now is a lot of small pages showing in your view screen (see Figure 5).
- Go to the "Insert" menu on the top tool bar.
- Slide down to "Picture" and "From File"
- Go to your "My Pictures" files (or wherever you saved your picture) and open the picture you want to use.
- Click OK (or Insert, if using a Mac).
- Your picture should be showing on your Excel page (see Figure 6).

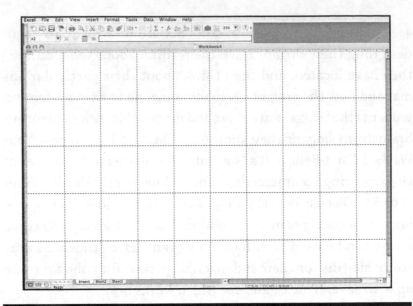

Figure 5. Excel document example.

Figure 6. The Excel document with the picture inserted.

Now the students can size their pictures to meet their needs:

- Click on the picture to make sure it is selected (the handles— little squares—should be showing around the edges).
- Click on the right bottom corner square and drag until the picture is the size you want (a good poster size is about 2 x 2 pages or 3 x 2 pages).
- Now go to "File" and then select "Print Preview" to see how your enlarged picture will look. You'll see that parts of it will print on different pages. That's fine. However, make sure the picture still looks clear—not too fuzzy. If it is beginning to look really fuzzy, you may want to choose a different picture.

Students should now add their slogan:

- Now use WordArt to add your slogan.
- You can use the "Insert" menu → Picture → WordArt, or you can use the Drawing toolbar, which looks like a large capital letter A tilted a little to the right.
- A small window will pop up (see Figure 7). This is where you select the style of lettering that you want. Be sure to pick a style that will be easy to read from a distance. Sometimes the 3-D effects tend to blur the words and they're not as easy to read.
- Once you click on the style you want, another window pops up (see Figure 8). Here you can type in the text that you want for your slogan. You also can choose the font you want to use.
- Hint! WordArt doesn't make a line break for you, so think about where you want the words to go and where you want a break. Be sure to hit the "enter" key where you want to make a new line. Remember that you can always go back later and change it if you don't like the way it looks.

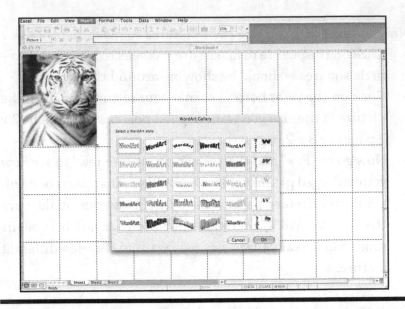

Figure 7. Select the WordArt you'd like to include.

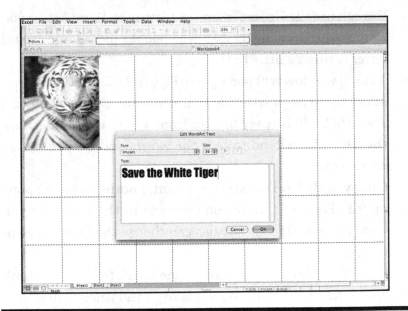

Figure 8. Type in your slogan text.

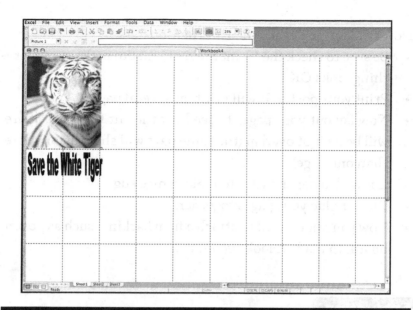

Figure 9. Adding the slogan to the poster.

- Now that your WordArt is on the page, you'll probably need to adjust the sizing. Make sure it is selected, and then use the handles to adjust the width or height to fit your picture. The colored handles let you turn and adjust the tilt of the words.
- You also can adjust the colors of your WordArt. For example, the style you chose may have had yellow, but yellow doesn't go with your picture. Make sure the WordArt slogan is selected, then click on the formatting button on the Drawing tool bar. Under Fill, you'll find many color choices. You'll also see "More Fill Colors" and "Fill Effects." Fill effects lets you choose a blend of several colors. You also can use patterns, some premade backgrounds, or you can even choose a picture you already have for the fill.
- Now select your slogan, and place it on the poster where you think it will look best. It can be below the picture in a white space if that's what you want (see Figure 9).

Now students are ready to print their posters:

- Be sure to check the "Print Preview" first to make sure everything looks OK.
- Print your poster. It will print on several pages.
- Now lay out your pages to see how they fit together. There will be a bit of overlap (the same part will show up on more than one page).
- Cut with a paper cutter to make a nice edge.
- Tape or glue your pages together.
- Now you might want to attach a firm backing, such as poster board, to make it look even nicer.

Evaluation

Posters will be assessed according to the following criteria:

1 = attempt to meet criteria
2 = partially meets criteria
3 = meets or exceeds criteria

Poster reflects a sympathetic view of the selected animal	1	2	3
Poster is colorful and easy for audience to see	1	2	3
Slogan is original and creative	1	2	3
Slogan is able to communicate the desired message	1	2	3

Summary

Students have created an excellent tool to use as part of their persuasive presentation. Posters can be printed on ordinary printer paper, but if you can afford the photo paper or better quality paper, they will be glossier and even more impressive.

Alternative Lesson: Creating a Podcast

A great way to expand your audience for student work and to increase student motivation with an authentic audience is to have students create a podcast. If you Google the terms "create podcast," you'll find a wealth of resources that provide directions to help you create your own unique broadcast.

After locating the perfect picture to represent their campaign and developing their posters, the students' persuasive speeches can be presented as a podcast. If you have access to a Mac with GarageBand, you can create podcasts in just a few easy steps. Podcasts can be audio, audio with pictures, or video when using GarageBand software. Sound effects and music easily can be added and edited. If you are using another format, you'll need to prepare everything to be ready in "real time" because editing may not be an option. The following lesson steps can be followed when using GarageBand for an audio podcast with pictures or adapted for other methods.

1. Find samples of good student podcasts through iTunes or the Internet. Audio clips are much different than the kind of media students typically see with lots of visual clues. Students should listen for examples of:
- clear speech;
- interesting voicing, like good "read-aloud" voices;
- interesting and creative language that engages the audience; and
- how sound effects and music can be used effectively.

2. Students should prepare their campaign speeches, keeping the above in mind, and have the electronic versions of their posters ready to go. They also should rehearse their speech (reading or memorized) several times so that it sounds natural. They can do this in partners reading to each other. They then should read for the teacher when they believe they are microphone ready.

3. Open a "New Podcast Episode" on GarageBand (or go to the Internet site of your choice for podcasting; http://audacity. sourceforge.net is student-friendly), create a quiet atmosphere, and begin recording. In GarageBand, it's easy to edit, erase, start over, and eliminate mistakes, but even in other podcast creators, you can develop a great product. If working in GarageBand, students can easily take turns reading their own persuasive speeches. Music and sound effects can be added later.

4. Each of the animal photos located earlier need to be saved in iPhoto. In GarageBand, the photos can then be dragged into the podcast track and placed at the appropriate spot. They will show as the podcast is played.

5. If the podcast is created on the Web, it's already to go. Just follow directions for broadcast (RSS) and you're set. In GarageBand, you'll need to upload the podcast so that it can be shared with others. The method you use will depend on its Internet location. You may need a converter to change the file to an MP3 (audio) or MP4 (audio plus pictures or video) file so that anyone can access and listen to it. This can be done through a free online file converter such as those found on http://media-convert.com or http://zamzar.com.

6. Invite the audience to subscribe to the podcast. It can be downloaded through tools like iTunes, or just posted to a Web site for listeners to locate.

Suggested resources for creating podcasts include:
- Gcast (http://www.gcast.com)
- MyPodcast (http://www.mypodcast.com)
- Podbean.com (http://www.podbean.com)
- podOmatic (http://www.podomatic.com)

Jamestown: An Historical Role Play

By Kenneth J. Smith, Ph.D.

Grade Level

Grade 3, but it could easily be adapted to grades 4–12.

Overview

In the early 1600s, England's King James I, son of Mary, Queen of Scots, and (it is thought) her assassinated husband, inherited the English throne from Elizabeth I. His ascension was not well received by the English citizenry, and Elizabeth left James with virtually no financial reserve and no ability to raise taxes. Thus, in 1607, James, short on cash and envisioning himself as King of the "New World," established the colony of Jamestown in Virginia. The students will be developing a television program based on these historical figures.

Objectives

The following objectives are based on National Educational Technology Standards, as well as national content area standards in language arts and social studies.

1. Students will understand the political, religious, and social institutions that influenced James's ascension to the throne and the establishment of Jamestown.

2. Students will understand the interconnection between the strengths and foibles of the central historical figures.
3. Students will understand the causes and connections among varying Native American responses to the colony.
4. Students will understand the historical personal and public difficulties of being the leader of a country.
5. Students will understand class and economic struggles that influenced decision making at the time.
6. Students will locate relevant reference points on a map.

Standards Met

Social Studies and History

1. Students understand why the Americas attracted Europeans and how Europeans struggled for control of North America and the Caribbean. (Students incorporate the historical background of different European countries and monarchs.)
2. Students understand how political, religious, and social institutions emerged in English colonies. (Students examine the establishment of the colony from the point of view of commoners, members of the gentry and nobility, and the Native Americans. Moreover, they integrate the respective, concomitant religious view of each group.)
3. Students understand how the values and institutions of Europe economic life took root in the colonies. (Students discuss the economic goals that drove individual and governmental motivations.)

4. Students understand family life now and in the past, and family life in various places. (Students examine family roles in the different class systems.)
5. Students demonstrate an understanding that different people may describe the same event or situation in diverse ways, citing reasons for the differences in views. (Students explain the same empirical events from the point of view of the different people and cultures involved and discuss why each presents these events differently.)
6. Students demonstrate an understanding that different scholars may describe the same event or situation in different ways but must provide reasons or evidence for their views. (Students examine various print and online sources, comparing and contrasting different accounts.)
7. Students investigate, interpret, and analyze multiple historical and contemporary viewpoints within and across cultures related to important events, recurring dilemmas, and persistent issues. (Students discuss empirical events from the point of views of different cultures involved, using first-person arguments to present different perspectives.)

Technology

1. Students are proficient in the use of technology.
2. Students use technology tools to enhance learning, increase productivity, and promote creativity
3. Students use telecommunications to collaborate, publish, and interact with peers, experts, and other audiences.

English Language Arts

1. Students read a wide range of print and nonprint texts to build an understanding of texts, of themselves, and of the cultures of the United States and the world; to acquire new information; to respond to the needs and demands of society and the workplace; and for personal fulfillment. Among these texts are fiction and nonfiction, classic and contemporary works. (Students use online and print sources as well as a variety of graphics.)

2. Students conduct research on issues and interests by generating ideas and questions, and by posing problems. They gather, evaluate, and synthesize data from a variety of sources (e.g., print and nonprint texts, artifacts, people) to communicate their discoveries in ways that suit their purpose and audience.

3. Students use a variety of technological and information resources (e.g., libraries, databases, computer networks, video) to gather and synthesize information and to create and communicate knowledge.

Materials

- Tom Snyder Productions Timeliner XE (http://www.tomsnyder.com/timelinerex/index.asp)
- iMovie (for Macintosh computers only)
- Video camera
- Regular access to computers
- Information from a variety of sources, including fiction, biographies, and downloadable maps (e.g., http://www.atlapedia.com)

- handouts
- pictures

Procedure

1. Students, after having learned about the start of the colony, are told about Mary and Elizabeth's tempestuous relationship. This is presented in storytelling fashion—almost as if it were a soap opera. Major themes include the conflict between Catholics and Protestants, opposition to female rulers, the desires each had to rule England, and the irony of Mary's son inheriting Elizabeth's crown. Students should be given a questionnaire about the story that they complete in small groups. Groups then compare and discuss answers until they agree upon one correct set of answers. For homework, they are to write a set of questions stating what more they want to know about the people.

2. Have students go online to see pictures of the main "characters" in this story. They should discuss what the clothing reveals about the person's values. They are given an overview of the television program they will produce and told that they will bring important objects to the taping that reveal insights into the life and values of the person they will portray. They begin reading encyclopedia and downloaded articles about each person. (These cannot be read online, as they need to be edited by the teacher ahead of time for sexual content that is deemed age inappropriate.) For homework, students should write quizzes and answer keys about the historical figures.

3. Students are given a blank family tree of the main figures. They are told, again in storytelling fashion, about significant

people that connected Mary with Elizabeth (e.g., Henry VIII, Mary I of England). Students complete the family tree as the story unfolds. For homework, they are to memorize the tree.

4. Students use the names on the family tree to create bingo-like card for a game called JAME-O. They are given first person quotes and must decide which historical figure on the card most likely said the quote (e.g., "No I won't help you cousin, but I have a lovely room you can stay in—for the next 17 years.") For homework, students are to write five more quotes (students never seem to tire of this game). Students also are given a matching sheet of key events and dates that they will, at a time of their own choosing, need to take as a quiz.

5. Students work in small groups to create Venn diagrams comparing and contrasting two historical figures. Students choose one and write an acrostic poem using the person's name (e.g., King: **K**ing of Scotland at age 1; **I**reland took his attention away from Jamestown; **N**orth Ireland is the section of the country he tried to take over; **G**ot mad at Parliament).

6. Students should begin listing symbolic objects for each character to show on the TV program (e.g., jewelry, Bible, bill rejected by Parliament to raise taxes, invitation to a party). They will work in small groups to rank these in order of importance. For homework, they assume the role of a historical figure and write a letter to another person during that time. The letter must reveal some action the figure took that affected history.

7. Have students read their letters aloud in class and write answers to each other. They then role-play other figures telling their version of the same story.

8. Students will debate each historical figure's most significant flaw. Next, they will debate each person's most difficult decision he or she was faced with.

9. Students will use Timeliner 5.0 to show the eight most significant events in one of the historical figure's life. The definition of *significant* is left open for them to decide. For homework, they will make or draw something that belongs to a character and bring it to show and tell.

10. Have students mark significant events and travels their figure took on a map.

11. Students will need to decide which character they will be for the TV show and determine what format they'd like it to be (e.g., talk show, newscast, etc.). Because this is a group project, multiple groups may do the same type of show, because each will have a different perspective and script. The students will role-play their historical figures using information they've gathered from research throughout this unit. Groups should spend a few days preparing for their TV shows before the final production. The goal of the TV show is to highlight the interpersonal and historical conflicts of the time.

12. Record the students as they conduct their TV show.

13. After the students have completed their TV shows, they will use iMovie to edit the video. In many ways, this proves the most challenging aspect of the project. They must decide the most important interpersonal and historical conflicts and then debate throughout the compilation/editing process which moments best capture these conflicts.

False Faces

by Angela Ardoin

Grade Level

Grade 5

Overview

Students will learn about folktales through Native American storytelling. They will write their own folktale and design a mask to represent it. Students will take what they have learned from the lesson and put it into a movie form, explaining how their folktale came about and what the mask represents. This lesson should last 4 to 5 class sessions.

Objectives

1. Students will write and illustrate a folktale.
2. Students will utilize the folktale to create a movie.
3. Students will design a mask.

Standards Met

History

1. Students understand comparative characteristics of societies in the Americas, Western Europe, and Western Africa that increasingly interacted after 1450.

2. Students understand how early European exploration and colonization resulted in cultural and ecological interactions among previously unconnected peoples.

English Language Arts

1. Students use spoken, written, and visual language to accomplish their own purposes (e.g., for learning, enjoyment, persuasion, and the exchange of information).
2. Students adjust their use of spoken, written, and visual language to communicate effectively with a variety of audiences and for different purposes.

Materials

- Construction paper (various colors and sizes)
- Scissors
- Glue
- Sequins, beads, glitter, and the like for decoration of the masks
- An Internet-accessible computer running Windows
- Microsoft Windows Movie Maker
- PALM handheld computers with Sketchy™ program (one per student)
- Projector
- Flex camera
- Various types of masks to put around the room or photos of masks
- CD of tribal drums
- Poster paper and marker

- Resources (e.g., books, videos, encyclopedias)
- Stapler and staples

Procedure

1. Display various types of Native American masks around your room. If you do not have access to actual masks, you can post pictures of them instead. Play a tribal drum CD as students are entering the room or as an attention getter at the beginning of the lesson.

2. On the poster paper, begin a KWL chart (What I **K**now, What I **W**ant to Know, What I **L**earned). Ask students what they already know about Native Americans, folktales, and mask making. Next, ask students what they want to know about Native Americans, folktales, and mask making. Post the chart on the wall and have students refer to it during the unit.

3. Allow students to research the above topics using the Internet, encyclopedias, and various other resources.

4. Have students search the Web for slide shows and images of Native American masks.

5. As a class, have students complete the What I Learned section of the KWL chart and make sure that all What I Want to Know questions have been answered.

6. Hand out the PALMs and have students use the Sketchy™ program to write and illustrate their own folktale. (For this project, it is helpful to have students help create the rubric because

they seem to understand what is expected and its purpose better when they help develop it. It also gives students a chance to verbalize their expectations of each other and the teacher can check for understanding as well.)

7. Once students have completed their folktales, have them come to the teacher station (projector connected to a computer and a flex camera) and present their Sketchy™ folktale to the class.

8. Using their folktales as inspiration, students will design a mask depicting the story. Briefly explain the importance of symmetry in mask making. To create the masks:

- Have students fold a piece of construction paper lengthwise and draw half of an oval, which then should be cut out. This will create the facial shape.
- Unfold the oval and starting at the top center, cut a one-inch slit. Then move to the bottom center and cut another one-inch slit.
- Fold the left flap over the right flap and staple. Do this to both the top and bottom slits. This will cause the facial shape to "pop" out.
- Staple the edges of the facial shape to a larger piece of construction paper.
- Have students cut out the eyes, mouth, and nose using construction paper and glue these to the facial shape.
- Once the features are in place, students may decorate as they please to have the mask depict their folktale.

9. Using Microsoft Movie Maker, have students create a movie about their folktale. If they are artists, have them draw their own pictures, scan them in, and use them in the movie. If they sing, have them perform a song for the background. If they love

to perform, have them act out the folktale and video it. They should use the program to edit their video. Have a movie night during which students introduce their movies and art to the community.

Evaluation

Sample rubrics are included in Figures 10 and 11.

False Faces Folktale

Movie Maker Rubric

Criteria	100% of aspect is present 4	75% of aspect is present 3	50% of aspect is present 2	25% of aspect is present 1	0% of aspect is present 0
Movie is completed on time.					
Folktale is apparent and depicted well in the movie.					
Information is correct.					
Movie includes transitions.					
Movie includes a title slide.					
Movie includes a credit slide.					
Link to Native American culture is apparent.					
Music is included.					
Photos are included (include at least one of mask).					
Works cited page was turned in to teacher.					
Contains a brief explanation of how the mask fit into the folktale.					

Scoring: 44–41 = A; 40–37 = B; 36–33 = C; 32–29 = D; 28–0 = U

Student: _____

Teacher Comments: _____

Figure 10. False Faces Movie Maker rubric.

False Faces

Mask Rubric

Criteria	100% of aspect is present 4	75% of aspect is present 3	50% of aspect is present 2	25% of aspect is present 1	0% of aspect is present 0
The mask was completed on time.					
The mask had a Native American look, indicating that the student had used Web sites and other appropriate sources to help design it.					
The mask was neatly and attractively made.					
Student can explain the connection of their mask to their folktale.					
Symmetry is evident.					

Scoring: 20–17 = A; 16–14 = B; 13–11 = C; 10–8 = D; 7–0 = U

Student: _____

Teacher Comments: _____

Figure 11. False Faces mask rubric.

States Within the U.S.: Making Connections:

By Sandra Cookson

Grade Level

Grade 6

Overview

Students will be assigned a state and asked to write a report. The report is to include information in the following areas: population and area; climate and terrain; industry and resources; educations; careers; government; state symbols; major cities; and famous people. A concept map will be used to help students make connections among the information needed. By organizing the information into a web, students will see the connection between the key points and details of the report. At a later point, hyperlinks will be added to the report to facilitate the connections between seemingly unrelated facts. The topic for research is the state, but the real focus is on the research process. Strategies for organizing and presenting information will be at the heart of each lesson.

Objectives

1. Students will learn about the unique history of their state and how events in world and U.S. history shaped the history of their state.

2. Students will become more familiar with the geography of the United States.
3. Students will understand how the resources available in their state have affected the economy of the state.
4. Students will understand the relationships among the various factors of their state and how they relate.
5. Students will use technology tools to make physical connections of related information within a written report.

Standards Met

English Language Arts

1. Students conduct research on issues and interests by generating ideas and questions and by posing problems. They gather, evaluate, and synthesize data from a variety of sources to communicate their discoveries in ways that suit their purpose and audience.
2. Students use a variety of technological and information resources to gather and synthesize information and to create and communicate knowledge.
3. Students read a wide range of print and nonprint texts to build an understanding of texts, of themselves, and of the cultures of the United States and the world; to acquire new information; to respond to the needs and demands of society and the workplace; and for personal fulfillment.
4. Students employ a wide range of strategies as they write and use different writing process elements appropriately to communicate with different audiences for a variety of purposes.

5. Students apply a wide range of strategies to comprehend, interpret, evaluate, and appreciate texts. They draw on their prior experience, their interactions with other readers and writers, their knowledge of word meaning and of other texts, their word identification strategies, and their understanding of textual features.

Technology

1. Students demonstrate a sound understanding of technology concepts, systems, and operations.
2. Students use critical thinking skills to plan and conduct research, manage projects, solve problems, and make informed decisions using appropriate digital tools and resources.
3. Students apply digital tools to gather, evaluate, and use information.

Materials

- Word processing program (such as Microsoft Word)
- Drawing program
- Internet access
- Research materials

Procedure

In addition to writing the report using a word processing program, students will make a concept map or Web and create an interactive report using links and anchors to connect related topics within the report.

1. Students will use word processing software to learn proper format and spacing for a research paper. Explicit instruction should be given around the use of indents, quotations, and parenthetical references, consistent with MLA format. In an effort to give the written report interactive capabilities, students need to be taught to make anchors using key words and how to link those key words to another location within the text. A major focus of successful linking involves understanding the organization of the files within a single folder. This should be an explicit, planned lesson and should be reinforced through the writing process.

2. Also known as mind maps, webbing is used to help students organize a variety of information they are being asked to include in their reports. To help organize students, break up the required information into five easy-to-manage categories using the four pillars of social studies (geography, civic government, economics, and history), plus a fifth (people). With the state name at the top of the web and five category headings lined up beneath, students should place the required information into the web together as a class.

3. Students should discover that some topics fall under more than one category. For example, *industry* and *resources* may belong under "Economics" and "Geography." With the basic skeleton completed, students then begin their research filling in their own webs with specific information about their assigned state.

4. As students begin to plug information into their webs, instruction should be given around skills such as aligning text boxes, placing connectors, and using font size and attributes to convey

importance and subordination. The importance of good note taking becomes evident during this process as students make choices about which information should be included in the web and which details to leave for the body of the report. For the interactive report, the web serves as a "Table of Contents" in which the viewer can click on any given topic and link directly to that portion of the report.

Evaluation

For the web and interactive report, students self-evaluate prior to final viewing by a teacher. The rubric should evaluate four key areas: the presence of a single folder to contain all linked files; mechanical aspects of writing, including the use of spell-checker and appropriate font size and color; and technical aspects of writing, including word choice.

Summary

By making the physical conditions between the facts and information in their reports, students are able to see real-world connections inherent in the details. The use of these connections also facilitates the process of writing their papers and makes the information within their writing flow much more fluently.

Shapes Are All Around Us

By Sharon Leamy

Grades 5–6

Overview

Geometry is a very visual branch of mathematics, requiring students to grasp the concepts of one-, two-, and three-dimensional figures. These concepts can be more firmly understood by identifying the forms in real-life objects.

The textbook unit on geometry at this level will cover lines, angles, polygons, circles, and transformations. Definitions, measurements, relationships, and proper mathematical notation and vocabulary will be included as well.

The project presented here is a culmination of the unit. Working in teams, students will be required to draw, photograph, and label geometric shapes from the world around them. These observations will be compiled into a PowerPoint presentation to be shared with the rest of the class.

Objectives

1. To develop students' knowledge of geometry, including lines, angles, polygons, and transformations.

2. To develop students' use and understanding of precise mathematic vocabulary to explain geometric shapes, measurements, and relationships.
3. To introduce the concepts and tools of shape measurement and relationships.
4. To introduce the concepts and types of transformations.
5. To help the students see the use of geometry in the real world.

Standards

Math

1. Students will measure length, capacity, weight/mass, and angles using sophisticated instruments (e.g., compass, protractor, trundle wheel).
2. Students will apply the concepts and attributes of length, capacity, weight/mass, perimeter, area, volume, time, temperature, and angle measures in practical situations.
3. Students will select and apply instruments including rulers and protractors and units of measure to the degree of accuracy required.
4. Students will use concepts of symmetry, congruency, similarity, scale, perspective, and angles to describe and analyze two- and three- dimensional shapes found in practical applications.
5. Students will identify, describe, classify, and compare two- and three-dimensional geometric figures and models according to their properties.

Materials

- Classroom math textbook
- Computers (one with a TV hook-up)
- Ruler
- Digital cameras
- Protractor
- Microsoft PowerPoint software
- Compass
- Scanner
- Drawing paper and pencils

Procedure

Lesson Outline

- Students will be divided into groups of 3–4. The project is to be a team effort, with equal contributions from each member.
- From a combination of student artwork and photographs of real-world objects, students are to identify examples of the following: one circle, three different types of angles, and four different types of polygons.
- Each shape is to be precisely and correctly identified and labeled.
- For the artwork, each student will compose a pencil drawing of any side of the school building, concentrating on the geometric shapes, rather than the artistry. The students should scan the pictures into the computer.
- Each student group will be allowed to take pictures from around the school grounds, using the school's digital cameras. Please remind students that no other classroom is to

be disturbed. The shots will be saved onto a disk until they can be loaded onto the computer.

- Each team will create a PowerPoint slide show displaying their examples. (Prior knowledge of PowerPoint software is assumed.) Along with the examples, the presentation must have both an introductory and closing slide. The closing slide must contain the names of the team members.
- Student teams will present their show to the rest of the class, in a 2–3 minute program. Each team member is to explain at least two of the examples.

Days 1–3

1. Divide the teams into thirds.

2. The first third of the class will stay in the classroom, using the computers. Each person will be on his or her own, reviewing the geometry section of the Web site Math.com (http://www.math.com/school/subject3/lessons/S3U1L4GL.html). The students are to follow steps 1–4 in each section, taking notes along the way.

3. The second third of the students will be positioned outside, along any wall of the school building. Each student is to do a pencil sketch of the building, focusing on the geometric shapes that make up the structure.

4. The final third of the students will walk around the inside of the school, selecting objects or places to photograph. (Rules for use of the camera will be thoroughly reviewed before the group begins.)

5. Rotate the groups so each student has a chance to complete all three activities.

Days 4–5

1. The groups will work together, deciding on examples, labeling and defining shapes, and creating their presentations.

2. Each group will work together at one computer.

3. Toward the end of Day 5, teams will be instructed to rehearse their oral presentation.

Day 6

1. The groups will share their presentations.

2. Hard copies of the presentations will be turned in to the teacher.

3. Assessment will be based on meeting the requirements outlined for the project.

Digital Vocabulary

By Eppie Snyder

Grade 8 (could be adapted for grades 6–8)

Overview

Using this lesson with gifted students encourages them to understand new vocabulary by using analysis and synthesis skills. It also is an avenue that allows the use of creativity and a nonroutine approach to language development and acquisition.

Objective

1. Students will acquire new vocabulary, either as stand-alone vocabulary or in conjunction with literary work.

Standards Met

English Language Arts

1. Students adjust their use of spoken, written, and visual language (e.g., conventions, style, vocabulary) to communicate effectively with a variety of audiences and for different purposes.

2. Students use a variety of technological and informational resources (e.g., libraries, databases, computer networks, video) to gather and synthesize information and to create and communicate knowledge.
3. Students participate as knowledgeable, reflective, creative, and critical members of a variety of literacy communities.
4. Students use spoken, written, and visual language to accomplish their own purposes (e.g., for learning, enjoyment, persuasion, and the exchange of information).

Materials

- Digital camera
- Computer
- Microsoft PowerPoint
- Printer (optional)
- Vocabulary words and definitions

Procedure

1. In a whole-group setting, review selected vocabulary words and meanings.

2. Divide students into manageable groups. (We suggest no more than four students to a group.)

3. Assign each group four or five vocabulary words.

4. Ask students to brainstorm ideas of how they could use these words in sentences that show their meaning. Students should write the sentences.

5. Now, introduce the ideas of "posing" in a manner that could illustrate the word in context.

6. Assign a schedule for using the digital camera (or hand out digital cameras to each group should you have access to more than one) and allow the students to take pictures illustrating their words in context.

7. After the images are saved, the group should import these pictures into a PowerPoint presentation and construct a sentence to use with each image incorporating the vocabulary word into the sentence. Often the group can use the original sentences that they created in their brainstorming activity. Sometimes those sentences must be modified to create the images. Sentences should be added to the presentation under each picture. (The teacher can create a template before beginning and students need only insert their pictures, type sentences, and save. This is advisable for first-time use or when doing this lesson with younger students. After the first time, students often design very creative presentations with less teacher involvement.) See Figure 12 for an example.

8. After completing their PowerPoint presentations, each group should present them to the class. Students assess each presentation, determine if the words are used correctly according to part of speech, and evaluate the value of each sentence and image.

Assessment

Have students design a rubric to assess each group's presentation. Alternatively, prepare an individual check sheet for each

Figure 12. Sample PowerPoint slide for "stymie."

student to use to evaluate each word during the presentation. A sample is included in Figure 13.

Summary

This strategy has been used as a part of a vocabulary development program to enhance and support richer writing and speech. Additional ideas include:

- Print the presentation and display on bulletin board.
- Share presentations with other classes to teach the vocabulary words. Involve the students as much as possible.
- Have eighth-grade students make presentations for younger students using their assigned vocabulary for the week.

Author's Note

This lesson was adapted from a presentation by Jeri-Lyn Flowers, Kim Poe, and Eppie Snider, and based on lessons taught by Jeri-Lyn Flowers.

Student Evaluation of Digital Vocabulary

Use the following scale: ++ superior, + excellent, 0 average, - needs work, -- redo it!

Vocabulary word: _____

_____ Picture was clear and easy to decipher.

_____ Sentence gave the viewer more information and helped to show meaning.

_____ Word was used correctly in the sentence.

_____ Sentence gave enough information to determine word meaning.

_____ Sentence was error free.

Evaluator's Name: _____
Date: _____

Figure 13. Student evaluation.

Making History

By David W. McDivitt

9–12

Overview

The 1930s were a turning point in world history. The problems of how to deal with the growing power of Adolf Hitler and Nazi Germany and the global depression were critical to the future course of the world. Czechoslovakia, France, Germany, Italy, United Kingdom, and the USSR played integral roles in the future of European politics. This unit will provide an opportunity for students to learn and experience the struggles of leading a country in times of economic and political toil using a computer-based simulation game.

Objectives

1. To teach students how Nazi Germany and Adolf Hitler affected the development of 1930s global politics.
2. To increase students knowledge of European geography.
3. To increase student understanding of the difficulties of being the leader of a country.
4. To teach students to successfully identify vocabulary of the unit.

Standards Met

History

1. Students will understand reform, revolution, and social change in the world economy of the early 20th century.
2. Students will understand the major global trends from 1900 to the end of World War II

Technology

1. Students will demonstrate introductory knowledge, skills, and understanding of concepts related to technology.
2. Students will demonstrate continual growth in technology knowledge and skills to stay abreast of current and emerging technologies

Materials

- Muzzy Lane software Making History: The Calm and the Storm (http://www.making-history.com/edu)
- Information including maps, handouts, and scenario information from Making History Gaming Headquarters (http://www.making-history.com/hq)
- Access to a computer for 3 days

Procedure

The following ideas are given for an optional assessment opportunity that students can do as homework while completing the in-class game. This is a good way to allow for student choice and authentic assessment.

Students will choose a project from the following list or create a project of their own with teacher approval. The project must address the people, places, culture, or events of this period in history.

- PowerPoint presentation
- Speech
- Essay
- Biography
- Game
- Model
- Flash Cards
- Web design
- Posters
- Collage
- Cultural food
- Maps

Procedure

1. *Day 1: Introduction.* The students will complete the following activities.

- *Activity 1* (35 minutes): Muzzy Lane Software (http://www.muzzylane.com) has been creating historically based strategic games that are being used in classrooms to introduce students to the concept of historical decision making. Making History: The Calm and the Storm (http://www.making-history.com/edu) places students in existing scenarios or challenges them to create new ones. This strategy game with a real-world scenario surrounding World War II introduces students to politics, the economy, and military scenarios. The game places students in decision-making roles using historical events to problem-solve solutions, and can be downloaded for a fee. Introduce the simulation "Making History: The Calm and the Storm" by demonstrating how to play via a computer/projector in the classroom. The teacher will need to have a good understanding of how to play the game prior to the demonstration, and will need to show students how to make treaties, raise and lower taxes, build and move military units, use the chat and journal features, and show how the game is scored. The teacher will distribute country goals and scenario overview and go over them with all students. Distribute a unit vocabulary list to students for review and announce a geography quiz.

- *Activity 2* (15 minutes): Pretest on 1938 European geography. Download map from http://www.making-history.com/hq. Copy the map and hand it out to students. Students will have 15 minutes to label as many countries as possible on the map. Students earn 1 point per correctly labeled country.

2. *Day 2: Classroom/computer lab (begin the game).* The students will complete the following activities.

- *Activity 1* (5 minutes): The teacher will announce the teams/countries for playing of the game. The teacher should stress that any communication between the teams/countries should be done via the chat feature of the game. Groups should stay together and not move about the computer lab. Dismiss class to the lab.
- *Activity 2* (35 minutes): Students will log on to the computers and join the game selected by the teacher. It is vital that the teacher understand how to set up multiple player games so the process will be quick and transition into playing the game will be smooth. Once the multiplayer game is established, then students will start the first turn. The teacher

should wander around the room to help students during the first turn. Encourage students to accomplish a task in all major areas of the game (diplomacy, finance, military, economics). Upon the completion of the first turn, save the game, have students log off, and use any remaining time to give student a short quiz over the unit's vocabulary.

3. *Day 3: Computer lab (let the fun begin)*. The students will complete the following activity.

- *Activity 1* (entire class period): The teacher will have students log in to the saved game and proceed to playing as quickly as possible. The teacher should use the turn timer feature in the game and set it to 10 minutes. The speed of the game will greatly increase and students should be busy trying to accomplish their countries' goals. At the end of the period, save the game and have student log off. The game should be through four turns by the end of Day 3.

4. *Day 4 (completion of the game)*. The students will complete the following activities.

- *Activity 1* (25 minutes): As on the Day 3, the turn timer should remain at 10 minutes. The game should come to completion during this class period.
- *Activity 2* (10 minutes): Upon completion of the game, have teams enter a journal via the software on the following topics: (1) Discuss the success and failure that your country experienced during this phase. (2) Discuss how your country could have done better in achieving its goals.
- *Activity 3* (10 minutes): Distribute and discuss for homework the "Discussion and Assessment Questions" downloadable from http://www.making-history.com/hq.

Assessment

The following activities should be used to assess students on this unit.

- *Activity 1* (10 minutes): Distribute the blank map from the Day 1 pretest and have students label the map again. Students will have 15 minutes to label as many countries as possible on the map. Students earn 1 point per correctly labeled country.
- *Activity 2* (20 minutes): Distribute "Key Thematic Questions" from http://www.making-history.com/hq and have student write complete answers to the questions.
- *Activity 3* (15 minutes): The teacher should lead a classroom discussion about the success and failures that occurred in the course of the game. The scoring features of the software will assist with this activity, as will the homework from Day 4 that has been collected.

Stop Motion Pro

By Rob Stetson

Grade Level

9–12

Overview

In the late 1970s, movies like *Star Wars* began using stop motion animation techniques for their motion picture production. For example, for a scene with the Imperial Walkers in *The Empire Strikes Back*, each frame of the animation is photographed separately as the subject is slightly altered between each photo. Then, the photographs are streamed in their original sequence to render an animated film. Students will be learning about and using this type of technology to make their own movie.

Objectives

1. To teach the students how to design a small background set and incrementally photograph each frame of an animated movie.
2. To increase students' knowledge of the motion picture industry.
3. To work in groups, focusing student attention on the value and execution of the process by treating it separately from the product.

4. To teach the students the Stop Motion Pro program so that they can see their individual photographs join together as frames in an .avi movie

5. To give the students different file management challenges: exporting, importing, and saving/opening to/from different drives and file servers.

6. To train students to become self-directed learners by having them learn the "how-tos" of how to be self-taught by following a tutorial.

Standards Met

Technology

1. Students demonstrate a sound understanding of the nature and operation of technology systems. (Demonstrate a sound understanding of how the digital camera and tripod is set up and used to successfully take and store a series of .jpg images.)

2. Students are proficient in the use of technology. (Teach uploading .jpg images to a computer and launching the Stop Motion Pro program so that the .jpg images can be sequentially streamed into MPEG formatted movie frames.)

3. Students use technology tools to enhance learning, increase productivity, and promote creativity. (Utilize the Stop Motion Pro animation technique to build and expand a creative frame of reference for developing and designing unique characters or subjects, first through the use of planning story boards, and then by a hands-on approach.)

4. Students use productivity tools to collaborate in constructing technology-enhanced models, prepare publications, and

produce other creative works. (Working in groups to collaborate in modeling a filmable set, complete with background, props, and character(s) with a constant focus of what the end product should be.)

5. Students use technology resources for solving problems and making informed decisions. (Research Stop Motion Animation Technology using Internet. Review articles on what it is, how it works, and which motion pictures used the technology (i.e., *Star Wars*). Use Internet and word processing technology to prepare and write a 250-word paper on the findings.

6. Students employ technology in the development of strategies for solving problems in the real world.

7. Students use technology resources for solving problems and making informed decisions.

Materials

- Raw material/s for making a character (e.g., clay, paper, sticks, wire, etc.)
- Downloaded trial version for Stop Motion Pro Software (http://www.stopmotionpro.com)
- Digital camera
- Tripod
- Microphone
- Computer

Procedure

1. Download and install a free trial version of the Stop Motion Pro software, found at http://stopmotionpro.com (choose "Cre-

ate Desktop ICON" during the Install Program). Students should utilize the tutorial found on that site when working on this project as a way to learn more about the program.

2. Have students make their own characters to be featured in their animation movies using clay, paper, sticks, wire, and other tools.

3. Students will take a sequence of digital photographs of their characters as they move or change the character by small increments. The camera resolution should be set to 640 X 480 pixels at a minimum.

4. Have the students upload their photos to a predetermined folder on the computer or CD-ROM. They will upload in the same sequence in which they were taken. Make sure the uploaded photos are numbered in order (e.g., pic001, pic002, pic003, etc.). If they aren't, rename them to follow the correct order.

5. Launch the Stop Motion Pro trial version.

6. Click OK to begin a new session.

7. Click OK to "Create a new project."

8. Type a "name" for the project, (keep it short, maybe only a few letters or the student's name) and click OK.

9. The "Capture Settings" dialog box will appear.

10. Select the "Directory Scan" option from the drop down menu.

11. Click on the "Browse" button and navigate to the folder that contains the images, double click on that folder name, and click OK.

12. Enter 640 for the pixel width (should agree with the resolution setting on the camera) and 480 for the pixel height (should agree with the resolution setting on the camera).

13. Make sure that the suffix is set to "JPG" and click OK.

14. Now, click "File/Import Individual Files . . ." (The folder containing the images should appear).

15. Select all images in that folder and click "Open."

16. A new window will appear, showing the images in sequence from first to last. Click OK. (The images will import into the Stop Motion Pro program, with the last frame showing.)

17. Click on the "Play" button to watch the movie.

Evaluation

Students' work can be evaluated using a rubric (see Figure 14).

Assessment Area	4	3	2	1	Score
Working in a Group Students are divided into groups to help teach the benefits of group work	*Effective Contributor* Proactive member, fully invested in project; works well with others	*Active Contributor* Participates in discussion and decision making; works with others	*Marginal Contributor* Somewhat engaged with group activities; makes a fair effort to work with others	*Ineffective Contributor* Little or no effort to work with others	
Vision of Project Can be assessed by observing brainstorming, having students submit a storyboard, or a written proposal, etc.	*Clear Vision* Clarity on where the project will go and how to get there	*Mostly Clear Vision* A basic idea of where project is going but still sketchy on how it will come together	*Somewhat Clear Vision* Fragmented idea of where project is going	*Poor Vision* Prefer to wing it, without any real plan, no real idea of what project will look like	
Time Management Give students time frames and deadlines to assess how well manage their time	*Managed Time Wisely* Met all deadlines by staying productive and performing equitable portion of the group work	*Managed Time Satisfactorily* Met most deadlines; tried to take on equitable portions of group effort	*Fair Time Management* Frequent idle time throughout project; unable to take on equitable portions of group effort	*Poor Time Management* Unable to meet deadlines; significant idle time throughout project	

Assessment Area	4	3	2	1	Score
Following Directions How successfully the student uses the tutorial to complete the project	*Excellent* Always tried the tutorial step first before asking a question; successful working off of the directions	*Good* Always tried the tutorial step first before asking a question; at least 80% successful working off of the directions	*Fair* Frequently asked questions without reading the directions first; at least 70% successful working off of the directions	*Poor* Unable or unwilling to follow directions.	
Demonstrate Knowledge of Technology	Full understanding of Stop Motion Animation software and how to convert to an .avi file	Adequate understanding of Stop Motion Animation software and how to convert to an .avi file	Some understanding of Stop Motion Animation software; able to convert to an .avi file with little or no help	Unable to use the Stop Motion Animation software; unable to convert to .avi file	
Product • Continuity • Creativity • Presentation	*Excellent Animation* Follow through of vision, very creative, technique of individual frames to result in excellent continuity; excellent presentation value	*Good Animation* Follow through of vision, shows creativity, enough frames to maintain continuity; satisfactory presentation value	*Fair Animation* Follow through of vision, lacking in frames and continuity; adequate presentation value	*Poor Animation* No vision realized, too few frames to have any continuity, deficient in substance; poor presentation value	

24–20 = A   19–15 = B   14–10 = C   9–5 = D 4 or less = F

Total _____

Figure 14. Stop Motion Pro movie project suggested rubric.

Images of Deceit

By Craig Wargowsky

9–12 (unit can be used as a cross-curricular project with social studies)

Overview

Art is more than studio work and technology is opening doors for the way we approach issues, especially in the classroom. This lesson allows students to delve into subjects using their imagination to make a statement on an issue. Using their art as a response, this type of lesson can encourage students to respond to historical and political events in terms of images. Humor, satire, or politics are used to convey their ideas. "Images of Deceit" is a visual expression of a student's perception on issues or response to a humorous situation using higher level thinking skills.

Our minds are constantly being exposed to visual images. With the world moving toward a more digital environment, people are seeing images broadcast over the Internet and other digital media. Viewers now need to decipher what is real, and what may be a fake or manipulated image. Some images are meant to deceive; some are used as propaganda, for editorial statements, or for simple humor. Students will view images using juxtaposition, as well as images meant to be deceitful.

After observing the images, students will have the opportunity to create a deceitful image.

Objectives

1. Students will understand and apply media, techniques, and processes using digital cameras and Internet search engines. Students will use Photoshop to create an image of deceit.
2. Students will choose an array of images, symbols, and ideas for their final image. The images should be used to convey a message in the final artwork.

Standards Met

Visual Arts

1. Students will understand the use of manipulated images in relation to history and culture.
2. Students will formally critique and assess the characteristics and merits of their work and the work of others.
3. Students will make a connection between visual art's practice of manipulating images and the practical use in other disciplines and professions.

Technology

1. Students will demonstrate a sound understanding of the nature and operation of technology systems. Students will demonstrate proficiency in the use of technology.

2. Students will use technology tools to enhance learning, increase productivity, and promote creativity in production of work.
3. Students will use a variety of media and formats to communicate information and ideas to multiple audiences.
4. Students use technology to locate, evaluate, and collect information from a variety of sources.
5. Students will use technology resources for solving problems and making informed decisions.

Materials

- Adobe Photoshop CS2 (or later versions)
- Available search engines such as Google, Yahoo, and MSN
- Kodak Easy Share 5 megapixel cameras (or similar digital cameras)
- 516-megabyte memory card
- 516-megabyte jump drive
- Access to a computer for 5 days
- LCD projector for demonstrations
- Color printer
- Paper (preferably a heavy weight or cardstock)
- Mat board
- Mat cutter

Procedure

1. *Day 1: Introduction.* Students will complete the following activities.
   - *Activity 1* (10 minutes): Students will be shown a PowerPoint presentation showcasing juxtaposed, fake, altered, funny,

and deceiving images. Students will see how digital media can be used to alter images.

- *Activity 2* (20 minutes): Students will brainstorm ideas for their own project. Projects can be political, editorial, funny, or deceiving. Students need three ideas written down to discuss with the teacher before leaving class. During this time, students will be using a search engine for ideas and inspiration. Students can save available images to their jump drives.
- *Activity 3* (20 minutes): Using digital cameras, students will take a picture, using features such as zoom and crop, and learn to delete. Once finished, each student should meet with the instructor to approve an idea for manipulation.

2. *Day 2: Loading and preparing images to manipulate.* Students will complete the following activities.

- *Activity 1* (10 minutes): Students will be shown how to save images to their school account (or CD-ROM). They will learn how to open the images in Adobe Photoshop and convert the image to a JPEG.
- *Activity 2* (40 minutes): Students will begin to load their collected images to their computer. Students can insert the memory card from the camera onto the computer. All images will be loaded onto the students' school accounts and saved in a folder titled "Image of Deceit" (or saved onto a CD-ROM). Once loaded, images will be opened in Adobe Photoshop and converted to JPEG files. All image resolution needs to be changed to 200.

3. *Day 3: Introduction to the basic Photoshop tools.* Students will complete the following activities.

- *Activity 1* (25 minutes): Students will observe a demonstration on the basic tools of Photoshop, which include the marquee, eyedropper, eraser, brush, magic wand, polygonal lasso, move, type, zoom, and paint bucket tools. Students will be encouraged to try other tools, but are expected to become fluent with the tools demonstrated.
- *Activity 2* (25 minutes): Students will experiment with the Photoshop tools, testing the techniques on their saved images.

4. *Day 4: Beginning of image manipulation.* Students will complete the following activity.
- *Activity 1* (50 minutes): Students will begin manipulating their images. Focus should be on deleting any unwanted parts of their image, and saving all work as a Photoshop document (PSD).

5. *Day 5: Manipulation of image.* Students will complete the following activity.
- *Activity 1* (50 minutes): Students will continue to alter their images, and begin to crop, copy, paste, and combine their images. Students will once again save all work as a PSD.

6. *Day 6: Completion of manipulation and printing.* Students will complete the following activities.
- *Activity 1* (up to 40 minutes): Students will finish the manipulation of their image, and show it to the teacher. Once the picture has been approved, it should be saved as a JPEG (see Figures 15–17 for examples).
- *Activity 2* (remainder of class): Once works are saved as JPEG images, the students can print their images. Images should be no bigger than 4 inches by 6 inches. Once images are

Figure 15. Image taken with a digital camera and altered on Adobe Photoshop CS2. Artwork by Megan Yost.

Figure 16. Image taken with a digital camera and altered on Adobe Photoshop CS2. Artwork by Ryan Monroe.

Figure 17. Image taken with a digital camera and altered on Adobe Photoshop CS2. Artwork by Kelsey Leimeister.

printed, they must be matted. Students will use the mat cutter for matting, and then display their image.

7. *Day 7: Critiquing and connecting.* Students will complete the following activities.

- *Activity 1* (30 minutes): Students will complete a written critique of each other's artwork. They each will be assigned an artwork to critique, and using learned vocabulary, will be asked to identify two things the artist did well, and two things the artist could improve.

- *Activity 2* (20 minutes): Students will write a brief reflection of the project, focusing on what tools they used and how those tools could be applied to careers or real-life situations.

Assessment

Students should be graded based on a rubric designed by the teacher that measures elements and principles of art and design.

Creating a Utopian Society

By Diane Witt

Grade Level

10–12 (students with high interest in writing and technology)

Overview

The search for the ideal society is ongoing and comes from the Greek words *utopia* (meaning "good place") and *outopia* (meaning "no place"). The two words evoke thoughts, hopes, and dreams of a society where individuals make the world a better place.

This 6-week unit addresses the study of a utopian society 100 years in the future where students will confront challenges to their freedoms based on perception, imagination, and literature. Today's technology will be the vehicle for decisions pertaining to leadership and the creation of a "New World Order." Web tools like Wikispaces at (http://www.wikispaces.com), Pbwiki (http://pbwiki.com/academic.wiki), Persuasion Map (http://www.readwritethink.org/materials/persuasion_map), and Teen Second Life (http://teen.secondlife.com) are the tools that will help students make decisions about the current society. When teams have finished their writing, they will be asked to present their scenario of the society, discuss the characters, and read their edict.

Subjects covered in this unit are future studies, science fiction, and social change. Literature can provide insight into this unit. Students should have read at least one of the following prior to the beginning of the unit.

1. Thomas More's *Utopia*
2. Lois Lowry's *The Giver*
3. Aldous Huxley's *Brave New World*
4. Kim Stanley Robinson's *The Mars Trilogy*

Objectives

1. To develop writing skills associated with collaboration.
2. To use the Internet to collaborate with peers at the local, regional, national, or international level.
3. To build upon history and literature of past societies to create a new one.
4. To create a future scene that reflects creativity, forward thinking, and flexibility demonstrated by working together.
5. To create a decree for the people regarding this new society, that uses technology tools to convey the message.

Standards Met

Social Studies

1. Students use knowledge of perspectives, practices, and products of cultural, ethnic, and social groups to analyze the impact of commonality and diversity within local, national, regional, and global settings.

2. Students use knowledge of the rights and responsibilities of citizenship in order to examine and evaluate civic ideals and to participate in community life.
3. Students use economic reasoning skills and knowledge of major economic concepts, issues, and systems in order to make informed choices as producers, consumers, savers, investors, workers, and citizens in an interdependent world.
4. Students use the knowledge of the purposes, structures, and processes of political systems at the local, state, national, and international levels to understand that people create systems of government as structures of power and authority to provide order, maintain stability, and promote the general welfare.
5. Students collect, organize, evaluate, and synthesize information from multiple sources to draw logical conclusions. Students communicate this information using appropriate social studies terminology in multimedia form and apply what they have learned to societal issues in simulated or real-world settings.

English Language Arts

1. Students critique the effectiveness and validity of arguments in text and whether they achieve the author's purpose.
2. Students synthesize the content from several sources on a single issue or those written by a single author, clarifying ideas and connecting them to other sources and related topics.
3. Students analyze an author's implicit and explicit philosophical assumptions and beliefs about a subject.

4. Students compile, organize, and evaluate information; take notes; and summarize findings.
5. Students use style guides to produce oral and written reports that give proper credit for sources (e.g., words, ideas, images, and information) and include an acceptable format for source acknowledgement.
6. Students communicate findings, reporting on the substance and processes orally, visually, and in writing or through multimedia.
7. Students determine a purpose and audience and plan strategies (e.g., adapting formality of style, including explanations or definitions as appropriate to audience needs) to address purpose and audience.
8. Students use available technology to compose text.
9. Students define and investigate self-selected or assigned issues, topics, and problems. They locate, select, and make use of relevant information from a variety of media, reference, and technological sources. Students use an appropriate form to communicate their findings.
10. Students gain information from reading for purposes of learning about a subject, doing a job, making decisions, and accomplishing a task. Students need to apply the reading process to various types of informational texts, including essays, magazines, newspapers, textbooks, instruction manuals, consumer and workplace documents, reference materials, multimedia, and electronic resources. They learn to attend to text features, such as titles, subtitles, and visual aids to make predictions and build text knowledge. They learn to read diagrams, charts, graphs, maps, and displays in text as sources of additional information. Students use their knowledge of text structure to organize content information, analyze it, and draw inferences from it. Strategic

readers learn to recognize arguments, bias, stereotyping, and propaganda in informational text sources.

Definitions

- *Persuasion Map*: An interactive graphic organizer that lets students plan their strategy for a persuasive essay or debate.
- *Teen Second Life*: Teen Second Life is for teens between the ages of 13 and 17. It is a place where teens can meet, play, and interact with other teens their age. This virtual world is made up of teens from all over the world where they build buildings, vehicles, and societies using their imagination.
- *Flip Books*: The flip book was a low-tech device that became animated as you flipped the pages. They had their beginnings when movies were being introduced. Now, with the computer, flip books can be made with little effort. To make a flip book, students will need a printer, digital camera, staples, rubber bands, and glue. Students should:
  1. Take a series of pictures on continuous mode using a digital camera.
  2. Plan the flipbook so pictures are aligned and the same size. Numbering the pages can make it easier to keep them in order.
  3. Using a desktop publishing program or photo-editing program, students should lay out the flip book pages, making sure they have a different picture on each sheet.
  4. Use white paper to print the flipbook. Cut out the individual frames. Print the pictures and glue them to stiff paper (Curtin, 2007).

Procedure

This unit is designed to have students confront the problems of a society based on their perception of the future. They will need to ask questions of themselves pertaining to leadership and whether or not they will be protectors of a way of life or dominators of a new order.

Inhabitants of the Utopian society will be faced with an edict for change. What is the greatest challenge facing their country or world? What are some solutions? What does their world look like? Who are the main characters? Is there any opposition to this Utopian decree? If so, how will they be handled?

Divide the class into teams. Teams should consist of no less than four and no more than six students. Each team will need to write a narrative outlining its society, the successes and challenges, and how its society functions. Team members should identify someone to be responsible for each part of the project, but each member is expected to contribute.

The unit will integrate wikis, Teen Second Life, and a persuasion map to convey students' vision. They also will have the option to create an animated flipbook to further demonstrate their characters if the school does not allow the use of Teen Second Life.

The wiki format forms the basis for this project. The teacher can use Wikispaces (http://www.wikispaces.com) or PbWiki (http://pbwiki.com/academic.wiki) for students to author their characters. In addition to the wiki, Teen Second Life (http://teen.secondlife.com) will be used to take the project into the virtual world. Although Teen Second Life is only accessible for teens, adults are allowed on the premises as long as they agree to a background check and agree to all of the rules. Teen Second Life will be used to integrate the "New World Vision" as students see it. Students also can use Persuasion Map (http://www.readwritethink.org/materials/persuasion_map), podcasts, and YouTube to convey their message to their audience. Although some schools have opted out of using Teen Second Life, the Web site is taking precautions to make sure that children are safe. Parents and teachers can act as volunteers in this virtual world to ensure safety of the students. Along with the background check of all adults who will be participating, parents will probably need to authorize a permission slip from the school granting permission for their child to access Teen Second Life in the classroom.

Groups need to think about many aspects of their utopian society from the beginning of this project. Students need to plan their characters (the people living in this society), as well as think about the society's "current" situation (remember, this utopian society is something that exists 100 years from now) and issues that may affect it. Sample questions students may want to consider are listed below.

Character Development

1. Who are the fictional characters in your society? (Teams should develop at least four.)
2. What are the characters' interests?
3. What role does your character play in the new world (e.g., hero, concerned citizen)?
4. What are the characters' strengths and weaknesses?
5. What kinds of personalities would these people have?

The Current Situation

1. What is the current society like?

2. Is there conflict? Can it be controlled and how?
3. What role does technology play in the life of these individuals?
4. Who wants this new society and who does not?

Issues That May Affect the Utopian Society

1. Free enterprise
2. Travel
3. Cultural diversity
4. Varied interests
5. Free will
6. Energy
7. Currency
8. Tolerance for change
9. Orderly system
10. Individual goals and perceptions

As they began planning their society with these questions in mind, the groups will begin developing their characters in their wiki and Teen Second Life. It often is helpful to create an outline to keep the team on track. Realize that the writing is ongoing and visions and perceptions of the developing project will change as time goes on. Using an outline will help to keep the team organized and also act as a roadmap as the project continues. An example is shown below.

Character 1

   A. Name and title

      1. Short bio

      2. Belief system

3. Another point
B. What does this person have to offer Utopia?
1. Point
2. Point
3. Point
C. How does this person fit into the overall picture?
1. Point
2. Point
3. Point

Each team will generate its own characters and plan out their vision for the utopian society, and each team member will contribute. Students will use a wiki to come to a consensus and formulate their ideas about their utopian society. They will integrate Teen Second Life to create their characters and build their society. After a basis for the society and the characters living there have been determined, the team will write a decree to outline their new world. They will use another venue, such as YouTube, to express their decree. The presentation can be placed online so audiences can view their work on the project.

Assessment

Students could be assessed with a rubric that focuses on the technology aspect of the project, the writing collaboration, participating in a group, and the like. The ability to work together as a team is no easy process and students should be aware that the group effort will play into their final grade. Originality and creativity can make or break any project. Make sure the team realizes the farther they go "outside the box" in their project development, the more they take ownership of their own work

References

Arbetman, L., & O'Brien, E. (1978). From classroom to courtroom: The mock trial. *Update on Law-Related Education, 2*(1), 13–15, 47–48.

Argetsinger, A. (2003, January 25). U-Md. says students use phones to cheat; text messaging delivers test answers. *The Washington Post*, p. B1.

Austega. (n.d.). *Characteristics checklist for gifted children.* Retrieved July 5, 2007, from http://www.austega.com/giftedcharacteristics.htm

Australian Government NetAlert. (2007). *A teacher's guide to Internet safety: How to teach Internet safety in our schools.* Melbourne, Australia: Australian Communications and Media Authority.

Barrett, H. (2002). *Introduction to electronic assessment portfolios.* Retrieved from http://electronicportfolios.com/ALI/intro.pdf

Belsey, B. (n.d.). *Cyberbullying: An emerging threat to the "always on" generation.* Retrieved April 4, 2008, from http://www.cyberbullying.ca/pdf/Cyberbullying_Article_by_Bill_Belsey.pdf

Callahan, C., & Kyburg, R. (2005). Talented and gifted youth. In D. L. DuBois & M. J. Karcher (Eds.), *Handbook of youth mentoring* (pp. 424–439). Thousands Oaks, CA: Sage.

Card, O. S. (2002). *Ender's game.* New York: Starscape.

Carlino, R. (2005). *How to work with virtual colleagues.* Retrieved January 16, 2006 from http://www.expatica.com/be/housing/relocation/how-to-work-with-virtual-colleagues-24659.html

Chen, M. (2002). *The virtual mentor.* Retrieved April 23, 2008, from http://www.edutopia.org/virtual-mentor

Children's Internet Protection Act, Pub. L. No. 106–554 (2001).

Christopher, M., Thomas, J., & Tallent-Runnels, M. (2004). Raising the bar: Encouraging high-level thinking in online discussion forums. *Roeper Review, 26*, 166–171.

Creating WebQuests. (n.d.). Retrieved November 22, 2008, from http://webquest.org/index-create.php

Curtin, D. (2007). *A short course book: Displaying and sharing your digital photos.* Retrieved from http://www.shortcourses.com/display/display3-8.html

Cybercitizenship.org. (n.d.). *What is cyberethics?* Retrieved November 21, 2008, from http://www.cybercitizenship.org/ethics/ethics.html

DeWitt-Heffner, J., & Oxenford, C. (2001). Defining the limits: CyberEthics. In *Annual proceedings of selected research and development and practice papers at the National Convention of the Association for Educational Communications and Technology, Atlanta, GA* (pp. 101–106). Retrieved from http://www.eric.ed.gov/ERICDocs/data/ericdocs2sql/content_storage_01/0000019b/80/1a/85/a9.pdf

EDUCAUSE Learning Initiative. (n.d.). *7 things you should know about . . . social bookmarking.* Retrieved November 22, 2008, from http://net.educause.edu/ir/library/pdf/ELI7001.pdf

Flanagan, B., & Calandra, B. (2005). Podcasting in the classroom. *Learning and Leading in the Classroom, 33*(3), 20–23.

Gamerman, E. (2006, January 21). Legalized "cheating." *The Wall Street Journal,* p. 1

Glod, M. (2006, September 22). Students rebel against database designed to thwart plagiarists. *The Washington Post,* p. A1.

Howard, R. M. (2000). Assigning collaborative writing: Tips for teachers. In G. Tate, A. Rupiper, & K. Schick (Eds.), *Composition pedagogies: A bibliographic guide* (pp. 54–71). New York: Oxford University Press.

Hubbard, J. (2007). *Educaching: A GPS-based curriculum for teachers.* Maumee, OH: SDG Creations.

Jackson, L. (2006). *Sites to see: Social bookmarking.* Retrieved November 25, 2008, from http://www.educationworld.com/a_techsites/sites.080.shtml

Jacobson-Harris, F. (2005). *I found it on the Internet: Coming of age online.* Chicago: American Library Association.

Johnson, D. (2003). *Learning right from wrong in the digital age.* Worthington, OH: Linworth.

Josephson Institute. (2002). *The ethics of American youth: 2002.* Retrieved November 24, 2008, from http://charactercounts.org/programs/reportcard/2002/index.html

Koterwas, T. (2007). *National School Boards Association research and guidelines on online social networking.* Retrieved November 21, 2008, from http://www.wdil.org/resources/national-school-boards-association-research-and-guidelines-on-online-social-networking

Lary, L. M. (2004). Hide and seek GPS and geocaching in the classroom. *Learning and Leading With Technology, 31*(6), 14–18.

Lathrop, A., & Foss, K. (2000). *Student cheating and plagiarism in the Internet era: A wake-up call.* Englewood, CO: Libraries Unlimited.

Lathrop, A., & Foss, K. (2005). *Guiding students from cheating and plagiarism to honesty and integrity: Strategies for change.* Englewood, CO: Libraries Unlimited.

Lenhart, A., & Madden, M. (2007). *Social networking Websites and teens: An overview.* Retrieved October 6, 2008, from http://www.pewinternet.org/PPF/r/198/report_display.asp

Levy, S., & Stone, B. (2006). *The new wisdom of the web.* Retrieved October 7, 2008, from http://www.newsweek.com/id45976/page1

Lipnack, J. (2001). *Virtual teams: The future is now.* Retrieved November 5, 2005, from http://www.linezine.com/72/articles/jlvtfin.ht

McCabe, D., Trevino, L. K., & Butterfield, K. D. (2001). Cheating in academic institutions: A decade of research. *Ethics and Behavior, 11,* 219–232.

McNulty, T. (2005, November 3). *American teens devour and feed Web's content.* Retrieved August 3, 2007, from http://www.pewinternet.org/PPF/r/301/press_coverageitem.asp

Mulrine, C. (2007). Creating a virtual learning environment for gifted and talented learners. *Gifted Child Today, 30*(2), 37–40.

Noble, S. (2008). *Team charter as part of project management training.* Retrieved from http://www.articlesbase.com/management-articles/team-charter-as-part-of-project-management-training-425676.html

O'Hear, S. (2006, August 8). *E-learning 2.0—How Web technologies are shaping education.* Retrieved from http://www.readwriteweb.com/archives/e-learning_20.php

Olsen, S. (2006, May 19). *Digital kids: Is technology injuring children?* Retrieved from http://www.news.com/ls=tech=injuring=children/2009-1041_3-607373

Olszewski-Kubilius, P., & Lee, S.-Y. (2004). Gifted adolescents' talent development through distance learning. *Journal for the Education of the Gifted, 28,* 7–35.

OTX. (2008). *Teens would rather have their lockers vandalized than homepage, but prefer shopping in store to online* [Press release]. Retrieved from http://www.toyassociation.org/AM/PDFs/Research/TeensAndInternet.pdf

Patrick, S. (2008). *Susan Patrick on online learning (school 2.0, part 9).* Retrieved from http://www.stevehargadon.com/2007/03/susan-patrick-on-online-learning-school.html

Popyack, J. L., Herman, N., Zoski, P., Char, B. W., Cera, C. D., & Lass, R. N. (2003). Academic dishonesty in a high-tech environment. In *Proceedings of the Thirty-Fourth SIGCSE Technical Symposium on Computer Science Education.* New York: ACM Press.

Prensky, M. (2007). *Simulation nation: The promise of virtual learning activities.* Retrieved from http://www.edutopia.org/print/3341

Rainie, L. (2008). *Trends in teen technology use.* Retrieved from http://www.pewinternet.org/ppt/2008%20_206.10.08%20-2020%20Children's%20online%20safety%20and%20literacy%20-%20pointSmart.ppt

Richardson, W. (2006). *Blogs, wikis, podcasts, and other powerful Web tools for classrooms.* Thousand Oaks, CA: Corwin Press.

Rimes, B. (2007). *Harry Potter lawsuit: You be the judge.* Retrieved from http://www.techsavvyed.net/?p+422

Rivero, V. (2005). At ease on a larger stage. *Telementor, 2*(5), 1–12.

Rowling, J. K. (1999). *Harry Potter and the chamber of secrets.* New York: Arthur A. Levine Books.

Schneider, J. (2009). Besides Google: Guiding gifted elementary students onto the entrance ramp of the information superhighway. *Gifted Child Today, 32*(1), 27–31.

Schwartau, W. (2001). *Internet and computer ethics for kids (and parents and teachers who haven't got a clue).* Seminole, FL: Interpact.

Schweizer, H., & Kossow, B. (2007). WebQuests: Tools for differentiation. *Gifted Child Today, 30*(1), 29–35.

Shaunessy, E., & Page, C. (2006). Promoting inquiry in the gifted classroom through GPS and GIS technologies. *Gifted Child Today, 29*(4), 42–53.

Siegle, D. (2002a). Creating a living portfolio: Document student growth with electronic portfolios. *Gifted Child Today, 25*(3), 60–63.

Siegle, D. (2002b). Learning online: A new educational opportunity for teachers and parents. *Gifted Child Today, 25*(4), 30–33.

Siegle, D. (2003). Mentors on the net: Extending learning through telementoring. *Gifted Child Today, 26*(4), 51–54.

Siegle, D. (2007). Podcasts and blogs: Learning opportunities on the information highway. *Gifted Child Today, 30*(3), 14–19.

Siegle, D. (2008). Working with wikis. *Gifted Child Today, 31*(1), 14–17.

Smith, R. O. (n.d.). *Learning in virtual teams: A summary of current literature.* Retrieved November 22, 2008, from https://www.msu.edu/~smithre9/Project12.htm

Stamatiou, P. (2005). *How to: Getting started with RSS.* Retrieved from http://paulstamatiou.com/2005/11/13/how-to-getting-started-with-rss

Sternberg, R. (1990). What constitutes a good definition of giftedness? *Journal for the Education of the Gifted, 14,* 96–100.

Titus, D. N. (1994, September). *Values education in American secondary schools.* Paper presented at the Kutztown University Education Conference, Kutztown, PA.

Trotter, A. (2008). *Educators get second chance.* Retrieved from http://www.edweek.org/ew/articles/2008/06/18/42secondlife_ep.h27.html?print=1

Valenza, J. K. (2003–2004). *Anti-plagiarism campaign: The struggle for academic integrity.* Retrieved from http://www.sdst.org/shs/library/pdf/plagiarismstory.pdf

United States Institute of Peace. (n.d.). *Guide to using simulations.* Retrieved October 30, 2008, from http://www.usip.org/etc/tools-resources/simulations/instructions.pdf

Utah Coalition for Educational Technology. (2008). *Geocaching and GPS in the classroom.* Retrieved from http://www.ucet.org/inUCETnew/

archives/2008/Conference/2008Presenters/ClintStephensGPS/
Geocaching%20Classroom%20Ideas.pdf

Wetzel, D. (2008). *Using wikis in science class: Teachers and students use educational technology to support learning.* Retrieved from http://www.suite101.comdaily.cfm/2008/09-08

What is a WebQuest? (n.d.). Retrieved November 22, 2008, from http://webquest.org/index.php

Willard, N. (n.d.). *Filtering software.* Retrieved November 2, 2008, from http://www.edu-cyberpg.com/Technology/filtering.html

Winter, E., Winter, J., & Emerson, S. (2003, October). *Will the real author please stand up?* Paper presented at the Preventing Plagiarism for Business Communication Annual Convention, Albuquerque, NM.

Young Adult Library Services Association. (n.d.). *Teens & social networking in school & public libraries: A toolkit for librarians & library workers.* Retrieved November 24, 2008, from http://www.ila.org/netsafe/SocialNetworkingToolkit.pdf

About the Author

DIANE **W**ITT has an undergraduate degree in design from Ohio University. She received her master's degree in special education and gifted education from Bowling Green State University in Ohio. She currently is employed as a gifted education consultant for the Ohio Department of Education. When not working, she enjoys traveling and gourmet cooking. Diane, her husband Scott, and their dog BeBe live in Ohio.

Author's Note

As I sat down to write this bio, I began to think about my journey through a diverse career in education. In past positions, I have employed a full-service approach to educating students with special needs, serving as an assistant, teacher, and coordinator. I am also the parent of an exceptionally gifted daughter and an advocate for children whose needs are not being met in the regular classroom.

Working with children whose abilities lie on both ends of the educational "bell curve" has strongly influenced how I view education. Education for me is fluid, adapting, and continually emerging in search for best practices. The search for a "way to do it better" as Edison once said leaves me open to change and possibilities.

For 10 years, my husband and I lived on Nantucket Island in Massachusetts, where I met a profoundly gifted young lady who opened up a completely new world of giftedness. Computer technology abilities connected everything together for her and allowed her to succeed. Regardless of their talents, gifted students need to find ways to reach for their vision. It is our responsibility to help them find their own voice.

About the Contributors

Angela Ardoin is a fifth-grade teacher at Dolby Elementary in Lake Charles, LA. She has received awards for her service, including the I-TEC Teacher-Model Technology Classroom Teacher award and the 2005 Louisiana Association of Computer Using Educators Elementary Teacher of the Year. She also is the school's Webmaster and technology contact. She has presented for numerous organizations, including the National Educational Computer Conference, the Louisiana Technology Showcase, and Economics Convention 2004. Ardoin is currently seeking a master's degree in educational technology.

Sandra Cookson is a technology and curriculum integration specialist in Orono and Veazie, ME. Through previous experience as a middle school classroom teacher and later a computer teacher in a K–8 school, Cookson developed a real passion for helping teachers find appropriate technology to support classroom objectives. Through the interactive nature of technology, lessons were adapted to meet students' interests and strengths, and provide practice and remediation when needed. In 2005, she was nominated for Maine's Technology Educator of the Year. It was this recognition and faith in her ability to work with peers to make a positive difference that lead Cookson to pursue a more formal role in developing, aligning, and delivering experiences that integrate technology with curriculum for the benefit of all students.

Jeri-Lyn Flowers is a graduate of the University of Georgia's Institute of Higher Education with a bachelor's degree in education. She received her master's degree from Kennesaw State University. Flowers holds National Board Certification and has taught for 15 years.

Sharon Leamy is fairly new to the teaching profession, having left the corporate world to earn her master's degree in teaching from Dominican University in May 2006. She began teaching sixth-, seventh-, and eighth-grade math and science in the fall of 2006 in Oak Park, IL. Leamy currently resides in Riverside, IL, with her husband and daughter.

David W. McDivitt currently is on staff at Oak Hill High School in Converse, IN, where he teaches world history and sociology. He is a 1993 graduate of Indiana University in Indianapolis, where he earned his bachelor's of science in education. He earned his master's degree in education from Indiana Wesleyan University in Marion, IN. McDivitt has been a high school social studies teacher for 12 years at Oak Hill, where he also serves as the defensive coordinator for the football team. He currently uses Muzzy Lane's Making History software in his World History classes. David is married to his lovely wife, Aileen, and together they have three wonderful daughters.

Debra Parkes lives in Columbus, OH. She graduated from Otterbein College with a bachelor of science degree in education. She has worked at The Wellington School, a coeducational, independent school, since 1995, where they promote lifelong learners and leaders. She has taught technology to pre-K through fourth grade for the past 5 years. She credits all of her accomplishments to her family because they are such extraordinary people. She is married to a wonderful, loving, supportive husband, Mike. She loves to laugh, read, travel, ski, play tennis, and watch the Ohio State Buckeyes beat any foe, especially the University of Michigan.

Kim Poe is a graduate of Kennesaw State University with a bachelor's degree in secondary education and English and a master's of education degree in middle grades. Poe has taught for 15 years.

Cindy Sheets is a gifted facilitator in Shawnee Mission, KS, where she has been teaching in an elementary gifted resource setting for the past 20 years. Her 12 years of service on the Board of Directors of the Kansas Association for the Gifted, Talented, and Creative has been spent serving as president, conference chair, and Web designer. She was elected to the NAGC Board of Directors as a teacher representative, served a 3-year term, and is currently serving on a national committee designing curriculum units for her students and integrating various forms of technology into the learning experience.

Kenneth J. Smith is the director of technology and enrichment for Sunset Ridge School District 29 in Northfield, IL. These two responsibilities, technology and enrichment, often complement each other synergistically. He has his Ph.D. in cognitive psychology from Columbia University in New York. Currently, Ken is working on a master's degree in clinical psychology, specializing in the social/emotional needs of gifted children. His most recent publications include an article in *Gifted Child Quarterly* on differentiating for gifted students in a heterogeneously grouped classroom and a short story in *Cricket Magazine*. This year, he was the Illinois recipient of the Larry Stilgebauer Award for Exemplary Use of Technology for the lesson featured in this book.

Eppie Snider is a graduate of Virginia Commonwealth University with a bachelor's degree in interior design and Berry College with a master's of education in middle grades and an Ed.S. in leadership. Snider taught for 9 years and currently is serving as an assistant principal.

Rob Stetson has worked in various computer technology capacities since he was aboard the U.S.S. Boston and asked to be transferred to data processing school in San Diego, CA. While waiting for his transfer, he chose Fire Control duty on the ship because that division had an analog computer. He eventually received the transfer he requested and went on to serve a 2-year tour of duty in London, England, as a Data Processing Technician. After returning to the United States, Stetson completed his college education. After 10 years working in industry, he decided to capitalize on his interests by preparing for a career in computer education. He is now completing his 12th year in public education and is currently employed at Nantucket High School as a computer teacher.

Craig Wargowsky teaches visual arts at Cuyahoga Falls High School in Cuyahoga Falls, OH. He is a 1999 graduate of Kent State University, where he earned his bachelor of science in art education. In 2006, he earned his master's degree in education (technology instruction) from the University of Akron. Wargowsky has been teaching art at Cuyahoga Falls since 1999, where he also worked as a basketball coach for grades 7 and 9. He currently uses Photoshop software and other digital media in his art classes. Since 2001, Wargowsky has been married to Heather, an elementary art teacher, and has a beautiful 5-year-old daughter, Leila, and a menacing 2-year-old son, Dylan. He plans on continuing his career teaching art and focusing of visual art practices in the advertising, business, and marketing world.

Printed in the United States
by Baker & Taylor Publisher Services

Printed in the United States
by Baker & Taylor Publisher Services